BEYOND A REASONABLE DOUBT

BEYOND A REASONABLE DOUBT

Herbert C. Casteel

COLLEGE PRESS PUBLISHING CO., Joplin, Missouri

Cover Photo:
Michael S. Morgan
Carthage, Missouri

Scripture quotes are from New International Version

Library of Congress Catalog Card Number: 90-80688
International Standard Book Number: 0-89900-351-6

Table of Contents

INTRODUCTION

Judges and trial lawyers deal constantly with evidence. It is the basic tool with which they work. They must be skilled in that vast body of law that is designed to assure that only reliable evidence finds its way into the trial of a lawsuit. The first thing a lawyer asks a client who is contemplating a lawsuit is, "Can you prove these claims you are making? What evidence do you have?"

But most people, including many Christians, are surprised to hear that evidence also is important to Christians. It is a common misconception that, while lawyers deal with facts, Christians deal with faith, and that there is no connection between the two. Rarely is a Christian asked, "Can you prove these claims you are

7

making? What evidence do you have?" Perhaps even more rare, is the Christian who can give a satisfactory answer when such a question is asked.

It has been said, only partly in jest, that "faith is something you believe that you know isn't true." Too many Christians profess a faith that is based on little more than emotion, and too many non-Christians have rejected Christianity because they believe it is based on little more than wishful thinking. In truth, Christianity is based on the strongest and soundest evidence ever provided to support any facts of ancient history. It is tragic that these facts are so little known. This book is organized into thirteen lessons to be used either by individuals or groups for a progressive study of the evidence which supports the truth of Christianity. The purpose is to strengthen the faith of Christians by showing that their faith is firmly based on historical fact and God-given truth. The book also is intended for non-Christians who have rejected Christianity as being unreliable or mythical.

Having spent fifteen years as a practicing attorney, plus twenty-six years as a trial judge, I naturally approach the subject from a lawyer's point of view. In effect I ask, "Can you prove these claims you are making? What evidence do you have?" My conclusion is, that not only is the Christian faith supported by sound evidence, but that evidence is sufficient to prove it to the highest degree required by law — beyond a reasonable doubt.

1

THE VITAL IMPORTANCE OF CHRISTIAN EVIDENCE

Christianity appeals to the intellect. The Bible repeatedly urges us to seek knowledge and wisdom from God, and to flee ignorance and superstition. Jesus told Paul that He was sending him to the Gentiles "to open their eyes and turn them from darkness to light" (Acts 26:18). The message which Paul took to the Gentiles was not some new philosophy, but was a factual account of events that had occurred at Jerusalem only a few years before – the death, burial, and resurrection of Jesus Christ. And because of these events, Paul urged the Gentiles to abandon their idols and superstitions and come to a new religion of truth and light.

It is important that we understand the uniqueness of Christianity. Some religions are based on the founder's claim to have received a private revelation from God; some are based on the founder's philosophy of life; some involve a method of thought control; some rely on obvious myths and fables. To such religions evidence is not important. But Christianity is different. For, "We did not follow cleverly invented stories when we told you about the power and coming of our Lord Jesus Christ, but we were eyewitnesses of His majesty." (2 Pet. 1:16)

Christianity is unique among the world's great religions in its claim to be based on historical fact testified to by many eyewitnesses. Evidence is of vital importance to a religion that makes such a claim. Christians claim that God actually has intervened in human history and that great events have occurred involving nations and governments and many people. As Paul said in his defense before King Agrippa, "The king is familiar with these things, and I can speak freely to him. I am convinced that none of this has escaped his notice, because it was not done in a corner." (Acts 26:26)

Some Christians are uncomfortable with a study of Christian evidences. They feel that such a study shows a lack of faith. But God does not call us to a blind faith. He calls us to an intelligent faith. God has provided the evidence and He has given us minds that are capable of understanding and evaluating that evidence. Surely He expects us to be diligent in our study of that evidence and to be honest in our evaluation. He wants our faith to be based on the firm foundation of historical truth.

JESUS' EVIDENCE TO PROVE HIS CLAIMS.

Jesus was careful to provide the evidence necessary

to give a firm factual foundation for our faith. After His resurrection He ate with the apostles, had them touch Him, and gave other proof that He was physically alive. "After His suffering, He showed Himself to these men and gave many convincing proofs that He was alive. He appeared to them over a period of forty days and spoke about the kingdom of God." (Acts 1:3)

Jesus often referred people to evidence that proved He was what He claimed to be, the Son of God. After John the Baptist was put in prison, he apparently became concerned as to whether or not Jesus was the long awaited Messiah and sent his followers to ask Jesus. Jesus referred them to the evidence. "Go back and report to John what you hear and see: The blind receive sight, the lame walk, those who have leprosy are cured, the deaf hear, the dead are raised, and the good news is preached to the poor." (Matt. 11:4-5)

To unbelieving Jews, Jesus also offered the evidence of His miracles. "I have testimony weightier than that of John. For the very work that the Father has given me to finish, and which I am doing, testifies that the Father has sent me." (John 5:36) He gave them further evidence by referring to the Old Testament prophesies that were being fulfilled in His life. "You diligently study the Scriptures because you think that by them you possess eternal life. These are the Scriptures that testify about me, yet you refuse to come to me to have life." (John 5:39-40)

When Philip asked Jesus to show them the Father, Jesus assured His disciples that anyone who had seen Him had seen the Father, and made this appeal to the evidence: "Believe me when I say that I am in the Father and the Father is in me; or at least believe on the evidence of the miracles themselves" (John 14:11).

11

After His resurrection, Jesus joined two disciples on the road to Emmaus who were in deep despair because this Jesus, whom they had hoped would be the Messiah, had instead been put to death. Jesus admonished them for failing to believe the Old Testament prophets and then gave them powerful evidence of His Messiahship by showing how scores of prophesies, made hundreds and even thousands of years before, had been fulfilled in His life and death. "And beginning with Moses and all the Prophets, He explained to them what was said in all the Scriptures concerning Himself" (Luke 24:27).

Since Jesus was careful to provide so much evidence for our benefit and made such frequent use of the evidence Himself, it is clear that a careful study of Christian evidences is vitally important to us.

EVIDENCES IN THE APOSTLES' PREACHING

The last instructions the apostles received from Jesus before He departed into Heaven stressed their role as witnesses. "But you will receive power when the Holy Spirit comes on you; and you will be my witnesses in Jerusalem, and in all Judea and Samaria, and to the ends of the earth." (Acts 1:8)

True to this command, the apostles went forth testifying as to what they had seen and heard during their time with Jesus. In the very first sermon preached to the new Church, Peter spent most of his time talking about the evidence for Christ's deity. He said "Men of Israel, listen to this: Jesus of Nazareth was a man accredited by God to you by miracles, wonders and signs, which God did among you through Him, as you yourselves know." (Acts 2:22) Note Peter's emphasis on the fact that many of his hearers had themselves witnessed these miracles, and that these miracles proved Jesus was accredited by God. Continuing in verses 24 to 31, Peter used the proof of fulfilled prophecy, quoting from Scriptures written a thousand years earlier by King David and fulfilled by the resurrection of Jesus. Finally at verse 32, Peter gave the eyewitness testimony of himself and the others with him of the fact that Jesus had risen from the tomb.

About three thousand people who heard this sermon, believed and were baptised that very day. Their faith was not a blind faith. They had heard evidence that was sufficient to convince any reasonable person that Jesus is the Christ, the Son of God. Their faith was an intelligent faith and the action they took was an intelligent response to that faith.

Other sermons recorded in Acts repeatedly make use of Christian evidences. For example, in his sermon at Antioch of Pisidia, Paul said, "The people of Jerusalem and their rulers did not recognize Jesus, yet in condemning Him they fulfilled the words of the prophets that are read every Sabbath." (Acts 13:27) Thus, not only were the ancient prophecies fulfilled in the life of Jesus, they actually were fulfilled unwittingly by the very ones who were trying to discredit and destroy Him. And as always, Paul appealed to the great evidence of the Resurrection. "But God raised Him from the dead, and for many days He was seen by those who had traveled with Him from Galilee to Jerusalem. They are now witnesses to our people." (Acts 13:30-31)

The extensive use of Christian evidences by the inspired apostles gives further proof of the importance of this subject for our study today.

EVIDENCE: ONE PURPOSE

The Gospel writers were inspired, not only to record the life and teachings of Jesus, but also to present evidence of His deity. Matthew was especially careful to show how Old Testament prophecies were fulfilled in the life of Jesus, frequently making such statements as:

> All this took place to fulfill what the Lord had said through the prophet: "The virgin will be with child and will give birth to a son, and they will call him Immanuel" — which means, "God with us" (Matt. 1:22-23).

Luke began his Gospel with this statement of purpose:

> Many have undertaken to draw up an account of the things that have been fulfilled among us, just as they were handed down to us by those who from the first were eyewitnesses and servants of the word. Therefore, since I myself have carefully investigated everything from the beginning, it seemed good also to me to write an orderly account for you, most excellent Theophilus, so that you may know the certainty of the things you have been taught (Luke 1:1-4).

John declared the purpose of his Gospel as follows:

> Jesus did many other miraculous signs in the presence of his disciples, which are not recorded in this book. But these are written that you may believe that Jesus is the Christ, the Son of God, and that by believing you may have life in his name (John 20:30-31).

14

In his first epistle, John explained the purpose of the New Testament writers as follows:

That which was from the beginning, which we have heard, which we have seen with our eyes, which we have looked at and our hands have touched – this we proclaim concerning the Word of life. The life appeared; we have seen it and testify to it, and we proclaim to you the eternal life, which was with the Father and has appeared to us. We proclaim to you what we have seen and heard, so that you also may have fellowship with us. And our fellowship is with the Father and with his Son, Jesus Christ. We write this to make our joy complete (I John 1:1-4)

Certainly if it were a purpose of the New Testament writers to present the evidence to us, it should be our purpose to study that evidence very carefully.

TWO GOALS OF THIS STUDY

By now it should be clear that God wants us to study Christian evidences. He wants us to have a firm factual foundation for our faith, so nothing can move us away from Him. In the fifteenth chapter of First Corinthians, after presenting evidence to prove that Jesus "has indeed been raised from the dead," thereby assuring us that our faith is not in vain, but is firmly grounded on historical truth, Paul concluded with this reasonable exhortation:

Therefore, my dear brothers, stand firm. Let nothing move you. Always give yourselves fully to the work of the Lord, because you know that your labor in the Lord is not in vain (I Cor. 15:58).

So one important purpose of this study is to strengthen our faith by giving us convincing evidence that the things we believe are true. This does not mean that feeling is eliminated and our faith consists solely of intellectual conviction. Love, joy, peace — the beautiful feelings that go with our faith are essential. The important thing to remember is that these wonderful feelings are the result of our faith — the fruit of the Spirit — and not the cause of our faith. Facts, not feeling, should be the foundation of our faith.

Feelings are vitally important to a Christian. They show that our faith is real and that the Holy Spirit dwells within. They are blessings that greatly enrich our lives. But our faith should be based on the facts, on the evidence, on God's truth. In the Parable of the Sower, Jesus said some seed fell on rocky ground and, because of shallow roots, withered away when the sun became hot. He explained this part of the parable as follows:

> The one who received the seed that fell on rocky places is the man who hears the word and at once receives it with joy. But since he has no root, he lasts only a short time. When trouble or persecution comes because of the word, he quickly falls away (Matt. 13:20-21).

We have all experienced times of discouragement when we have wondered if the things we believe are real. At such times, when our good feelings fail us, how important it is to know that our faith is deeply rooted in sound reason and the facts of history.

The other main purpose of a study of Christian evidences is to prepare Christians to witness to others. Even in the days of the apostles, people demanded

16

proof of the facts upon which Christianity is based. As the body of human knowledge has increased up to our own time, the demand for sound evidence has become more insistent. Plenty of evidence is available, but few are aware of its existence. Christians have a duty to supply that need.

> But in your hearts set apart Christ as Lord. Always be prepared to give an answer to everyone who asks you to give the reason for the hope that you have. But do this with gentleness and respect (I Pet. 3:15).

> Be wise in the way you act toward outsiders; make the most of every opportunity. Let your conversation be always full of grace, seasoned with salt, so that you may know how to answer everyone (Col. 4:5-6).

When people came to Jesus seeking the truth, He referred them to the evidence. The apostles did the same. When Christians are asked "the reason for the hope that you have," they should be prepared to "make the most of every opportunity." They should know the facts of history upon which Christianity is firmly grounded.

NOT EVERYTHING HAS TO BE PROVED

Because our faith is based on good evidence does not mean that everything has to be proved. Many things are not subject to proof. When Jesus tells us our sins are forgiven, or says He has prepared a place for us in Heaven, we believe Him because we trust Him. We trust Him because we are convinced He is the Son of God and we arrived at this conviction

17

because of the evidence. Martha shows the way in this in her conversation with Jesus after the death of her brother Lazarus.

> Jesus said to her, "I am the resurrection and the life. He who believes in me will live, even though he dies; and whoever lives and believes in me will never die. Do you believe this?" "Yes, Lord," she told him, "I believe that you are the Christ, the Son of God, who was to come into the world" (John 11:25-27).

It is doubtful that Martha fully understood what Jesus had said to her. But understand or not, she could quickly answer that she believed all that He said because she had already been convinced by the evidence that He is the Son of God.

Like Martha, when we are convinced by the evidence that Jesus is the Son of God, we believe all that He says whether we can prove it or not, or even whether we understand it or not. In like manner, when we are convinced by the evidence that the Bible is the Word of God, we accept all that it says, even those parts we cannot prove by direct evidence.

THE DEGREE OF PROOF REQUIRED

The study of Christian evidences is a study of matters of fact. Factual matters or events are not subject to absolute, mathematical proof. They are always subject to some possible doubt. For example, we all believe that George Washington was the first president of the United States. But it would be impossible to prove it beyond all possible doubt. The record in all the history books in the world could be doubted on the ground that history books do sometimes make mistakes. The inscriptions on all monuments could be doubted on the ground that inscriptions are sometimes in error. No matter what proof is offered, some possible doubt could be raised. But it is not reasonable to raise such doubts as to George Washington's presidency. It is not reasonable to expect any factual matter to be proved beyond all possible doubt. The highest standard of proof required in our courts of law is that required in criminal cases, where juries are instructed that they must find from the evidence that the defendant is guilty beyond a reasonable doubt. Upon such a finding a defendant can be sentenced to death. No greater proof is possible.

In our study of Christian evidences, we accept this same high standard. We will be looking for proof beyond a reasonable doubt. It is wrong to expect more. This is the mistake Thomas made when he refused to believe that the risen Lord had appeared to the other ten (John 20:24-25). Thomas had been with Jesus for three years and had seen plenty of evidence to show He is the Son of God; he had heard Jesus repeatedly predict His resurrection; he had heard reports of the resurrection from the women and others; he had probably been out to see the empty tomb; and he had the direct testimony of ten good men whom he had every reason to trust. Certainly this was ample evidence to prove the matter beyond a reasonable doubt. Thomas' doubt was unreasonable, and Jesus rebuked him:

> Then Jesus told him, "Because you have seen me, you have believed; blessed are those who have not seen and yet have believed" (John 20:29).

Jesus pronounced a blessing on those who would not demand a personal appearance, but with honest, open minds would consider the evidence and come to a reasonable decision. This is how we should approach our study of Christian Evidences.

Study Questions

1. Why is a study of evidences important to Christianity and not to other religions?
2. Explain why the Christian faith is an intelligent faith and not a blind faith.
3. Give an example of the use of evidences by Jesus.
4. What use of evidence did Peter employ in his sermon on Pentecost in Acts 2?
5. What use of evidence do you find in Peter's sermon at the temple in Acts 3:12-26?
6. What reason did Luke give for writing his Gospel?
7. What two things should we accomplish by a study of Christian evidences?
8. Why is it not necessary for everything we believe to be proved by direct evidence? How did Martha show us the way in this?
9. What degree of proof should we require? Explain why. How did Thomas error in this respect?
10. Why should our faith be based on facts, not feeling?

2

THE ISSUES AND THE OPPOSITION

The trial of a lawsuit is preceded by careful preparation. The rules of procedure permit each party to "discover" a great deal about his opponent's case. In this way the parties can identify the issues that must be presented to the jury, and can learn just who the opposition is, and just what claims the opposition makes. To avoid distracting the jury, a skillful attorney will weed out unnecessary details, and concentrate his efforts on those issues that really count.

Our study of Christian Evidences should be preceded by similar preparation. We need to define the important issues, and we need to identify the opposition. Who are the people who reject Christianity, and what do they offer in its stead? What evidence will we need to prove our case?

MOST PEOPLE REJECT CHRISTIANITY

The first thing we notice about the opposition could be very discouraging. Without a doubt the overwhelming majority of mankind do not believe the claims of Christianity. Furthermore, included among the unbelievers are most of the better educated people in the world today. Certainly this would cause Christians to question their own convictions, except for two very important facts:

1. Jesus told us it would be this way:

> Enter through the narrow gate. For wide is the gate and broad is the road that leads to destruction, and many enter through it. But small is the gate and narrow the road that leads to life, and only a few find it (Matt. 7:13-14).

Thus, despite the overwhelming evidence, which demonstrates the truth of Christianity, and despite Christianity's offer of rich blessings to all who will come, Jesus predicted that most people would reject it. The fact that this amazing prophecy has been clearly fulfilled, shows the divine foreknowledge of Jesus, and therefore strengthens, rather than weakens, Christian faith.

2. All this unbelief is based more on prejudice, emotion, and lack of knowledge, than it is on reason and sound evidence. And this is true of even the most highly educated unbelievers. It is not only possible, it is probable, that those graduating from most of the great universities in the world today, will have little

knowledge of the evidence for the truth of Christianity. Furthermore, much of this ignorance of the evidence for Christianity is deliberate. Again, Jesus, with His divine foreknowledge, predicted that it would be this way:

> This is the verdict: Light has come into the world, but men loved darkness instead of light because their deeds were evil (John 3:19).

Light is knowledge, and darkness is ignorance. Even well educated men and women avoid knowledge that might condemn the way they choose to live. Jesus said the evidence is readily available to anyone who chooses to do God's will:

> If anyone chooses to do God's will, he will find out whether my teaching comes from God or whether I speak on my own (John 7:17).

This is the basic cause of unbelief. In Chapters Five, Six, and Seven, we will consider the evidence that has been offered against Christianity, and will see its obvious weakness. In the other chapters in this book we will see the strength of the evidence in favor of Christianity. There is plenty of proof, but people do not want to believe. They seek to escape from God and His judgment because they do not want to change their life style. It suits their purpose for the world to have no meaning.

Aldous Huxley, in *Ends and Means*, Harper and Brothers, 1937, candidly admitted as much:

> I had motives for not wanting the world to have a meaning; consequently assumed it had none, and was able without any difficulty to find satisfying reasons for

23

matter of choice; not fact.

this assumption.

Most ignorance is vincible ignorance. We don't know because we don't want to know. It is our will that decides how and upon what subjects we shall use our intelligence. Those who detect no meaning in the world generally do so because, for one reason or another, it suits their books that the world should be meaningless (p. 312).

The philosopher who finds no meaning in the world is not concerned exclusively with a problem in pure metaphysics. He is also concerned to prove that there is no valid reason why he personally should not do as he wants to do, or why his friends should not seize political power and govern in the way that they find most advantageous to themselves (p. 315).

This is not to say that all unbelievers are bad people. Judged by human standards, many unbelievers are good people. But by God's standards they are rebellious sinners, creatures who defy and deny their own Creator. And the unbelievers philosophy of meaninglessness, that the universe is an accident and man is just a chance combination of chemicals, can lead to great evil. Any unselfishness exhibited by an unbeliever, is done in defiance of the unbeliever's own philosophy. Aldous Huxley in *Ends and Means*, page 313, said this concerning the atheistic philosopher, the Marquis de Sade:

De Sade's philosophy was the philosophy of meaninglessness carried to its logical conclusion. Life was without significance. Values were illusory and ideals merely the inventions of cunning priests and kings. Sensations and animal pleasures alone possessed reality and were alone worth living for. There was no reason why any one should have the slightest consideration for any one else. For those who found rape

24

and murder amusing, rape and murder were fully legitimate activities. And so on.

UNBELIEF IS EMOTIONAL

Not only is unbelief based on an amazing lack of knowledge, it also has a strong emotional content. Men do not come to the light because they love the darkness. (See John 3:19 above). People do not come to Jesus because they are emotionally attached to their own self-centered life style. They love to think that they are the chance product of evolution, and thus are not accountable to a Creator.

A very recent book, *Darwin on Trial*, Regnery Gateway, Washington, 1991, written by Phillip E. Johnson, professor of law at the University of California at Berkeley, recounts an incident which illustrates the strong emotional character of unbelief. In 1981 the British Museum of Natural History celebrated its centennial by opening a new exhibition on Darwin's theory. After asking the visitor to consider why there are so many different kinds of life, a sign stated, "The exhibition in this hall looks at one possible explanation — the explanation of Charles Darwin." A nearby poster stated that, "Another view is that God created all living things perfect and unchanging."

These seemingly innocent, and obviously true, statements, along with others in a similar vein, elicited a furious response from many prominent scientists. The managers of the museum were accused of having "lost their good sense" and even of giving support to Marxism. In the end the museum was forced to withdraw the offending statements.

Professor Thomas Barnes of the University of Texas, El Paso, told of a revealing incident that occurred on that campus. A lecture on evolution had been advertised, with the assurance that the speaker would answer questions at the end of his talk. Dr. Barnes attended the lecture and began asking questions that revealed obvious fallacies in the theory of evolution. The audience, composed of college teachers and students, became emotionally upset, with expressions of anger toward Dr. Barnes, and some even got up and left the meeting.

In truth, what Dr. Barnes was attending was not a scientific lecture and discussion, but instead a sort of pagan religious revival. The audience became angry because their faith was under attack. They loved the darkness and resented the intrusion of any light. But when unbelievers put aside their prejudice and emotion, and make an honest, intelligent study of the evidence, most will come to the light.

In a book entitled *A Lawyer and the Bible* written by a lawyer named I.H. Linton, the author tells how he encouraged other lawyers to study Christian evidences. Mr Linton stated he had never known of a lawyer who had made a careful, lawyer-like study of this evidence and remained an unbeliever. An English journalist named Frank Morison set out to prove the story of Christ's resurrection was nothing but a myth, but his investigation of the evidence caused him to place his faith in the risen Christ, and he ended up writing *Who Moved the Stone*, affirming the truth of the resurrection.

Many others have had similar experiences. Very few have made a careful, open-minded study of Christian evidences and remained unbelievers. Thus a

Christian's faith should not be threatened by the fact that most do not believe, nor should he be intimidated by the scholarship of some of the unbelievers. A true verdict is not rendered by a jury that refuses to listen to the evidence, or refuses to set aside its prejudices, or that imposes unreasonable standards of proof.

WHAT DO UNBELIEVERS BELIEVE?

In John, Chapter 6, is recorded some difficult teaching which Jesus gave to the crowd, with the following results:

> From this time many of his disciples turned back and no longer followed him. "You do not want to leave too, do you?" Jesus asked the Twelve. Simon Peter answered him, "Lord, to whom shall we go? You have the words of eternal life. We believe and know that you are the Holy One of God" (John 6:66-69).

Peter asked a good question. If men choose to reject Jesus, to whom shall they go? If men deny the Bible, where will they look for authority? If men turn away from God, where will they find the meaning of life? Those who refuse to believe the claims of Christianity — what do they believe?

Of course, unbelievers do not all believe alike. Some believe in no deity while others believe in a multitude of deities. Non-Christians include the other world religions with millions of followers and hundreds of cults, some with only a few followers. Many in America today, in a desperate search for meaning, have turned to Eastern cults of a pantheistic nature. Recognizing

27

the impossibility of explaining the universe on purely materialistic grounds, they add a spiritual dimension, but still avoid responsibility by claiming that God is all and all is God.

But to examine the beliefs and fallacies of all these religions and cults, would be to fall into an error that is avoided by any good trial lawyer. We must not become distracted with minor issues and lose sight of our real purpose. We must identify the real opposition so we can meet the real issues head-on. None of the other religions or cults makes any serious attempt or offers any evidence to disprove Christianity. Christianity claims to be the only God-approved religion. Jesus said that no one comes to God except through Him. Thus, if our evidence proves the claims of Christianity to be true, this necessarily disproves all the others.

THE REAL OPPOSITION: SECULAR HUMANISM

Without a doubt, the real opposition to Christianity today; that which would meet Christianity head-on and seek to disprove its claims, can be broadly defined as secular humanism. The numerous "isms" of unbelief can be most accurately grouped under this heading. The preface to the *Humanist Manifesto II* contains this statement:

> Many kinds of humanism exist in the contemporary world. The varieties and emphases of naturalistic humanism include "scientific," "ethical," "democratic," "religious," and "Marxist" humanism. Free thought, atheism, agnosticism, skepticism, deism, rationalism, ethical culture, and liberal religion all claim to be heir to the humanist tradition.

While all the adherents to these various "isms" do not agree on every issue, for our purposes it is fair to group them under the broad title of secular humanism. Humanists are an extremely powerful force in America today, having great influence in our educational systems, in our news and entertainment media, in our Federal judiciary, and in other areas of power. Dr. Francis A. Schaeffer in *A Christian Manifesto*. Crossway Books, Westchester, Illinois, 1982, emphasized the basic and irreconcilable conflict between Christianity and secular humanism in these excerpts from pages 19 to 21:

> When I say Christianity is true I mean it is true to total reality — the total of what is, beginning with the central reality, the objective existence of the personal-infinite God. Christianity is not just a series of truths but Truth — Truth about all of reality.

> Now let's go over to the other side — to those who hold the materialistic final reality concept. They saw the complete and total difference between the two positions more quickly than Christians. There were the Huxleys, George Bernard Shaw, and many others who understood a long time ago that there are two total concepts of reality and that it was one total reality against the other and not just a set of isolated and separated differences. The *Humanist Manifesto I*, published in 1933, showed with crystal clarity their comprehension of the totality of what is involved.

> They understood not only that there were two totally different concepts but that they would bring forth two totally different conclusions, both for individuals and for society. What we must understand is that the two world views really do bring forth with inevitable certainty not only personal differences, but also total differences in regard to society, government, and law.

There is no way to mix these two total world views. They are separate entities that cannot be synthesized.

At pages 112 and 113 of his book, Dr. Schaeffer describes the complete intolerance of humanism toward Christianity, and refers to humanist's efforts to make their world view the only one taught in our public schools:

> We must never forget that the humanistic position is an exclusivist, closed system which shuts out all contending viewpoints — especially if these views teach anything other than relative values and standards. Anything which presents absolute truth, values, or standards is quite rightly seen by the humanist to be a total denial of the humanistic position.
>
> As a result the humanistic, material-energy, chance world view is completely intolerant when it presents itself through the political institutions and especially through the schools.
>
> The humanistic, material-energy, chance world view intolerantly uses every form of force at its disposal to make its world view the exclusive one taught in the schools.

It is obvious that humanists recognize Christianity as their chief opposition, and are doing all they can to remove Christian influence from our culture. Through their control of textbook publishing, teacher's colleges, library selection, etc., they have practically eliminated any mention of the vital role of Christianity in our nations history. And our news media and our entertainment industry, who are normally careful to avoid offending any minority group, never hesitate to demean and ridicule the Christian faith. The fact that humanists see Christianity as their real opponent, confirms our view that the primary struggle today is between Christianity and secular humanism.

WHAT ARE THE ISSUES?

Having identified secular humanism as the main opponent of Christianity, now in our "pre-trial discovery," we need to define the issues. We can accomplish this by means of "interrogatories" to be answered by our opponent. For our answers, we will look to *Humanist Manifesto II*, published in 1973, and containing what is probably the most modern and most complete statement of the humanist faith. In this document, under the sub-title "religion," are the following:

> We find insufficient evidence for belief in the existence of a supernatural; it is either meaningless or irrelevant to the question of the survival and fulfillment of the human race. As non-theists, we begin with humans not God, nature not deity.

> . . . But we can discover no divine purpose or providence for the human species. While there is much we do not know, humans are responsible for what we are or will become. No deity will save us; we must save ourselves.

> . . . Modern science discredits such historic concepts as the "ghost in the machine" and the "separable soul." Rather, science affirms that the human species is an emergence from natural evolutionary forces. As far as we know, the total personality is a function of the biological organism transacting in a social and cultural context. There is no credible evidence that life survives the death of the body. We continue to exist in

31

our progeny and in the way that our lives have influenced others in our culture.

From these statements we can define the main issues as follows:

1. The existence of God.

According to the Christian faith, God does exist and He is the Creator of all things. He is eternal, all knowing, all powerful, and everywhere present. He gives purpose to our lives and meaning to the universe.

According to the humanistic faith, God does not exist; evolution is a scientific fact; and the universe has no meaning or purpose other than what we can give to it.

2. The existence of the spiritual realm.

According to the Christian faith, the spirit world does exist, and it is permanent, whereas the physical world is temporary. God is spirit, and by creating man in His own image, He made us spirit, and thus gave us individual worth. The spirit is eternal and lives on after the death of the body.

According to the humanistic faith, there are no spiritual things. Nothing exists except physical mass/energy. Human beings are nothing but the chemicals that make up the body, and nothing survives the death of the body.

3. The existence of supernatural things.

According to the Christian faith, the all-powerful God who created the universe and all of its "natural" laws, can and does intervene in His universe and, when it suits His purpose, does supernatural things.

According to the humanistic faith, supernatural events do not occur. Everything happens in keeping with the ordinary laws of nature.

4. The nature of the Bible.

According to the Christian faith, the Bible is the inspired Word of God, and as such it is completely true and accurate. It is accredited by the supernatural power of God through miracles and fulfilled prophecy.

Since humanism denies the existence of God and supernatural events, it follows that it denies that the Bible is inspired and denies its truth and accuracy.

5. The identity of Jesus.

According to the Christian faith, Jesus is the Christ, the Son of God. He was actually God in human form, and thus has shown us the true nature of God, rich in mercy and great in His love, and is worthy of our complete trust and confidence.

Since humanism denies the existence of God, it follows that it denies the deity of Jesus. If such a person existed, He was only a human teacher.

These then are the issues to which the evidence must be directed. First will come the evidence to prove that God exists, that the spirit world is real, and that supernatural events do occur. Proof of these issues will lay the groundwork for proof that the Bible is the Word of God and that Jesus is the Son of God.

We will also look at the evidence for the other side, which consists mainly of the opposition's efforts in the field of evolution. Because admission of special creation would force humanists to admit that God exists, they have devoted millions of man hours over the last 130 years in futile attempts to prove the theory of evolution. Because evolution is absolutely essential to the humanistic faith, they cling tenaciously to the theory, and use the Federal courts to maintain evolution's monopoly in our public schools.

Although *Humanist Manifesto II* speaks at great length about tolerance and the free exchange of ideas, humanists act vigorously and ruthlessly to suppress any teaching of creation science in our public schools, thus showing the vital importance of evolution to their faith, and showing their emotional attachment to humanism. Because of its great importance to our case, two full chapters are devoted to the evidence pertaining to evolution.

CONVERGING LINES OF EVIDENCE

Unlike other religions, Christianity may be proved or disproved, because, unlike other religions, Christianity is based on reason and historical fact. As we saw in Chapter One, Christianity invites and welcomes honest examination. In fact, Jesus and His apostles took the initiative in presenting evidence to prove the claims of Christianity.

Since we are dealing with questions of fact, the highest standard of proof possible is proof beyond a reasonable doubt, which is the highest standard required in a court of law. Lawyers seek to meet this standard by presenting converging lines of evidence, that is, by presenting as many different lines of evidence as possible, all of which point to the same fact.

How this works can be illustrated by considering the evidence in a typical burglary case. The victims are a rural couple who work in town. Upon return from work one evening, they find the back door of their home has been pried open. Missing are a 21 inch, Motorola television in a maple cabinet, and a General Electric micro-wave oven. The serial numbers are unknown. The pry mark on the door frame is 1¼ inches wide and contains red paint marks. A neighbor saw an older model, green pickup in the victims driveway on the day of the burglary. Make and model are unknown, but he did notice a large dent in the left fender and rust on the hood.

The sheriff remembers that defendant owns an older model, green pickup, and going to defendant's home sees the pickup in defendant's driveway. There is a large dent in the left fender and there is rust on the hood. This is important evidence pointing to defendant, but is not enough to prove guilt beyond a reasonable doubt. There are many older model, green pickups, and it is reasonable to believe that others may have large dents in the left fender and rust on the hood.

In the bed of defendant's pickup the sheriff sees a red pry bar. Its blade is 1¼ inches wide. Here is a second line of evidence pointing to the defendant. By itself it is not very strong, but taken together with the first line of evidence, it is more significant. It is reasonable to believe that very few people in the area own older model green pickups with large dents in the left fender and rust on the hood, and also own red pry bars with 1¼ inch blades. Still this should not be enough to find guilt beyond a reasonable doubt.

On defendant's back porch, the sheriff sees a 21 inch, Motorola television in a maple cabinet. The victims say it looks like their television. The defendant says some man whose name he does not know left it there for safe keeping. The sheriff finds a used furniture store in a neighboring town where defendant sold a General Electric micro-wave oven on the morning after the burglary. The victims say it looks like

35

their oven. The defendant says the same unknown man gave it to him for keeping his television. He doesn't know when the man will be back.

Note the cumulative effect of these four lines of evidence. Taken together, they are sufficient to prove the defendant's guilt beyond a reasonable doubt. The total is much more than the sum of the parts. In this study, look for converging lines of evidence pointing to the truth of all the issues listed above, and pointing ultimately to the truth of Christianity. You will find far more that four and thus a far greater cumulative weight of evidence. With an open mind, ask yourself if all these different lines of evidence, pointing inescapably to this great fact — Christianity is true — are not proof beyond a reasonable doubt.

Study Questions

1. Give two reasons why Christians need not be discouraged by the fact that most people do not believe the claims of Christianity.
2. Why do highly educated people often reject Christianity?
3. What do John 3:19 and 7:17 tell us about unbelief?
4. Why do some people choose to believe that life has no meaning?
5. What is the logical conclusion of the philosophy of meaninglessness?
6. What is the usual result when unbelievers make an honest, open-minded study of Christian evidences?
7. What is the real opposition to Christianity in America today and how have they become so powerful?
8. What are the main issues to be proved by Christian

evidences?

9. Why is evolution vitally important to secular humanism?

10. What is the significance of converging lines of evidence?

3

NATURAL THEISM, PART ONE

As we have seen, the primary struggle for men's souls in our country today is between Christianity and secular humanism. Atheism, agnosticism, and pantheism, while claiming to be different, all lead to a secular humanistic religion that denies God, or at least, denies any responsibility to Him. This chapter and Chapter Four, present evidence from Natural Theism for proof of God's existence and for the reality of the spiritual realm and for the truth of supernatural events. The terms "atheism", "unbelief", and "secular humanism" are used interchangeably.

Natural Theism is the science which treats of the existence and character of God in the light of nature and reason. This study will deal with proofs apart from the Bible and apart from historical and archaeological records. Can we find evidence of God and of spiritual things just by observing the universe and by using our own powers of reason? David, by inspiration of the Holy Spirit, wrote:

> The heavens declare the glory of God; the skies proclaim the work of his hands. Day after day they pour forth speech; night after night they display knowledge. There is no speech or language where their voice is not heard. Their voice goes out into all the earth, their words to the ends of the world (Psa. 19:1-4).

Certainly, as David said, the creation does declare the existence of a Creator, and this knowledge is available in all languages and in all parts of the earth.

Paul declared that the physical universe not only shows the existence of God, but also His eternal power and divine nature, and he said that men who ignore this and turn away from God are without excuse.

> For since the creation of the world God's invisible qualities—his eternal power and divine nature—have been clearly seen, being understood from what has been made, so that men are without excuse (Rom. 1:20).

In his speech to the Greek philosophers on Mars Hill, Paul appealed to their reason to show that God, who created the world, is Lord over all and is a spiritual Being who does not dwell in temples built by men, and does not need men to take care of Him.

> The God who made the world and everything in it is the Lord of heaven and earth and does not live in tem-

40

ples built by hands. And he is not served by human hands, as if he needed anything, because he himself gives all men life and breath and everything else (Acts 17:24-25).

Thus, not only is it proper to seek knowledge of God from nature and reason, it is clear that God expects us to do so. This chapter will be a study of the evidence we can see outside ourselves, that is from the universe around us. Chapter Four will deal with the evidence we can see within ourselves and from recent human experience.

CAUSE AND EFFECT

The principle of cause and effect is basic to our way of thinking. We cannot conceive of anything happening without being caused. When we see a brick wall we know that someone made the bricks, someone made the mortar, someone transported them to the work site, someone laid the bricks, and that someone had planned the whole project. Even if the wall just fell out of the sky, we would know that something caused it to fall. We would never believe the wall was just there without being caused by anyone or anything.

Furthermore, the cause must be an adequate cause. The effect cannot be greater than its cause. A wall containing 400 bricks cannot be built using only 200 bricks, nor can a creature having intelligence be made by a creator having no intelligence. And the cause must precede the effect. A brick wall cannot be built by a bricklayer who is not yet born, nor could the universe be created by one who did not exist before the universe.

41

With these principles in mind, we ask, "What caused the universe?" Three answers have been suggested: 1. The universe has in itself some natural process by which the universe has created itself. 2. The universe has always existed and thus was not created. 3. The universe was created by a supernatural power. What light can reason and nature shed on these suggested answers?

Reason tells us that answer number 1. is wrong, the universe did not create itself. To create is to cause to come into existence, that is, to make something from nothing. If, as secular humanism claims, nothing exists but the physical universe, then before the universe existed there was nothing, not even empty space, just non-existence. A natural law or process which is itself a part of the physical universe, could not have created the universe because before the universe existed the natural law did not exist either. A brick wall cannot be built by a bricklayer who is not yet born, nor can a universe be created by a natural law that is part of the universe and thus itself has not yet been created. The cause must precede the effect. Our reason and common sense tell us the universe did not create itself.

Nature also says that answer number 1 is wrong. Scientists tell us that the physical universe consists of energy and matter and that the two are interchangible. In other words, the universe consists of vast amounts of energy in one form or another. Wherever any process is taking place, energy is being transformed but none of it is being created or destroyed. Scientists call this the first law of thermodynamics. No one has ever discovered an exception to this law. No one has ever found any natural law or process that can either create or destroy even the smallest part of the physical universe. Man has never been able to breech that mysterious barrier between existence and non-existence. Nature, as expressed in the first law of thermodynamics, tells us that the universe did not create itself. There is nothing in nature, no natural law or process, that can create an atom, let alone an universe.

Now what can Natural Theism, that is, reason and nature, tell us about suggested answer number two? Reason tells us that answer number 2 is wrong also, the universe has not always existed. Atheists claim there is no such thing as the supernatural, but that everything operates according to natural laws, which human beings are capable of understanding. They claim the universe evolved from some eternal substance, such as "cosmic dust" or hydrogen gas, to its present state. But how could any such substance have neither beginning or ending? A math teacher was asked, "What is the largest number there is?" Her answer was, "I do not know. Only God could answer that." The teacher answered correctly. No natural law or human mind can solve the mysteries of eternity and infinity.

The story is told of an ancient Greek boy who asked his mother, "What is holding the earth up?" The mother replied, "There is a great strong man named Atlas and he holds the earth safely on his back." After a moment the boy asked, "What is Mr. Atlas standing on?" "Well son you have seen elephants in the victory parades. Atlas is standing on the back of a great strong elephant." Again after a moment the boy asked, "What is the elephant standing on?" "Son you have seen turtles and know they have hard shells and strong legs. Well the elephant stands safely on the back of the biggest turtle you can imagine." "But mother what is the turtle standing on?" "Well son it is just turtles all the way down. Now run out and play."

Obviously, cosmic dust or hydrogen gas all the way back is no more satisfying than turtles all the way down. Reason tells us there must have been a beginning. The universe is not eternal; it has not been here "all the way back." It is inconsistent to deny the existence of anything supernatural, and yet to claim that the universe has always been here. Anything that has always existed is not natural, it is supernatural. Only the supernatural God has always existed.

It is significant that Harvard University's world famous evolutionary astronomer, Dr. Harlow Shapley, effectively admitted that every effect must have a cause, that the cause must be antecedent, that is, must precede the effect, and that anything that has always existed is beyond natural explanation and thus is supernatural. In *The View From a Distant Star,* © 1963 by Basic Books, Inc. New York, Dr. Shapley stated:

> In the beginning was the Word, it has been piously recorded, and I might venture that modern astrophysics suggests that the Word was hydrogen gas. In the very beginning, we say, were hydrogen atoms; of course there must have been something antecedent, but we are not wise enough to know what. Whence came these atoms of hydrogen, these atoms, 20,000,000,000,000 (and 66 additional zeros) in number — atoms that we now believe have been forged into the material make-up of the universe? What preceded their appearance, if anything? That is perhaps a question for metaphysics. The origin of origins is beyond astronomy. It is perhaps beyond philosophy, in the realm of the to us Unknowable.

Thus, reason tells us that the physical or natural universe has not always existed. Anything that has always existed is beyond natural explanation. It is supernatural. Only God is eternal.

Nature also speaks against the eternal existence of the universe. Whereas the first law of thermodynamics says that energy is being neither created nor destroyed, the second law of thermodynamics says that energy is being degraded. The universe is running down. Energy is constantly being dissipated into space and becoming unavailable. This is a one-way process. Had the universe always existed, the running down process would be complete, and the universe would be cold and dead. Thus, there was a beginning. Nature says the universe has not always existed.

We are left with answer number 3, that the universe was created by a supernatural power. What can reason and nature tell about this? Reason says the universe is a great effect that had a cause. Reason also says that cause had to precede the universe and had to be greater than the universe. A natural law or process that is itself a part of the universe could neither precede the universe nor be greater than the universe. Thus the great cause of the universe must be something above and beyond the natural, it must be something supernatural. Since this great, supernatural cause has created creatures possessing intelligence, personality, self-consciousness, and free will, as well as sight, hearing, touch, and smell, this cause cannot be a blind, impersonal force. The great cause of the universe is a Person possessing all of the attributes found in the universe and much more, working in supernatural ways, and dwelling outside the physical universe in the spiritual realm. Reason says that God exists, that supernatural events do occur, and that the spirit world is real.

The great laws of nature also speak powerfully of a supernatural beginning for the universe. Creation is not a natural process. Man has never discovered any natural means for turning nothing into something, or even for turning something into nothing. Nature says that creation is a supernatural process. Nature also points to a definite beginning for the universe, a time when all the vast reaches of the universe, all the matter, energy, space, and even time itself, were brought into existence from non-existence. All of the one-way processes that men find in nature were set in motion, like a great clock, wound up and running down, and speaking clearly of a beginning and an ending. Truly, the heavens do declare the work of His hands, and He is clearly seen from the things that He has made. Nature tells us that the cause of the universe is a supernatural power; that the cause is God.

Unbelievers sometimes admit that they cannot explain where the universe came from, but argue that Christians are no better off because they cannot explain where God came from. But it is unbelievers who claim to have natural explanations for all things — a claim which they cannot back up. Christians believe the universe had a supernatural beginning — created by a supernatural God. Supernatural means above the natural and thus beyond our power to explain. Part of being a Christian is accepting the fact that man is not the greatest thing in the universe and that some things are beyond human understanding.

Oh, the depth of the riches of the wisdom and knowledge of God! How unsearchable his judgments, and his paths beyond tracing out! "Who has known the mind of the Lord? Or who has been his counselor?" (Rom. 11:33-34).

The universe is a great effect. The principles of cause and effect tell us that such an effect demands a cause and that cause had to precede the effect and be greater than the effect. Both reason and nature offer convincing proof that only a supernatural God could have been an adequate cause. It cannot be better said than this: In the beginning God created the heavens and the earth (Gen. 1:1).

DESIGN

Everywhere we look, from the vast universe itself to the tiny atom, we see intricate design. Design is evidence of intelligence, and intelligence is an attribute of personality. Thus, design not only tells us there is a Designer but also tells us something about the Designer — that He is a person possessing infinite intelligence and that He wants order and harmony. The evidence of design points not to some blind, impersonal force, but to God.

The great philosopher, Thomas Aquinas, saw proof of God's existence in the design of natural bodies. He is quoted as follows by Peter Kreeft in *A Summa of the Summa*, Ignatius Press, San Francisco, 1990, at page 69:

We see that things which lack intelligence, such as natural bodies, act for an end, and this is evident from their acting always, or nearly always, in the same way, so as to obtain the best result. Hence it is plain that not fortuitously, but designedly, do they achieve their end. Now whatever lacks intelligence cannot move towards an end, unless it be directed by some being endowed with knowledge and intelligence; as the arrow is shot to its mark by the archer. Therefore some intelligent being exists by whom all natural things are directed to their end; and this being we call God.

The unbeliever will object that given the vast expanse of space with billions of stars and planets, and given billions of years of time, all that we see in the universe came about by accident, by trial and error. A typical expression of this view is found in *The View From a Distant Star*, cited above. After theorizing that the universe began with a vast amount of hydrogen gas, Dr. Shapley wrote:

> Ordinary physics and astronomy suggest that if several billions of our years ago we had all that hydrogen and the natural physical laws, what we now see would have followed without the intervention of miracles, and without supernatural intercession. Gravitation, radiation, and eventually photosynthesis, genetics, and so forth — with operators such as these and the widely dispersed hydrogen atoms, the universe of galaxies, stars, planets, life, and man would have emerged — nothing supernatural required.

Of course Dr. Shapley cannot explain where the hydrogen atoms and all the natural physical laws came from, nor does he explain the obvious conflict of his theory with the second law of thermodynamics. He imagines a universe winding itself up instead of running down, as all observations show to be the fact. But passing over these problems for now, does Dr. Shapley's theory eliminate all evidence of design? Consider his tiny hydrogen atom. Programed into it had to be all the information and material needed to produce everything in the universe. Stars, oceans, mountains, light, electricity, plants, animals, hope, love — all this and billions more had to be packed into that tiny atom. What marvelous design that would have been. And what about the "natural physical laws" which are Dr. Shapley's "operators?" What marvelous operators indeed that could take nothing but hydrogen and construct every thing in the universe — again everything from galaxies to human love. In such laws as these, cannot even an unbeliever see evidence of intelligent design — evidence of a supernatural Lawgiver? No matter where the unbeliever starts, be it hydrogen gas or cosmic dust or anything else, he still cannot escape the evidence for design and the need for a Designer.

Furthermore, when we look at specific examples of design, it is hard to believe they are the accidental result of trial and error. Everywhere we look are found examples of design so intricate and so interdependent that they could have been produced only by supernatural intelligence and only according to a marvelous, overall plan. Specific examples of this, which will make this point abundantly clear, will be considered in the chapters on evolution. Certainly, the evidence of design speaks clearly of God, the all knowing, all powerful, supernatural Designer.

BEAUTY

There is a great deal of beauty in the universe. Human beings have the ability to appreciate and enjoy

49

this beauty. It is reasonable to believe this was planned. But who could have placed this beauty here and placed within us the corresponding ability to enjoy it? Certainly not a blind impersonal force, but an intelligent God who can enjoy beauty Himself. And this tells us something more about God – that He a good God who could look at His creation and see that it was good.

The unbeliever will object that beauty is in the eye of the beholder – that the universe ended up as it is accidentally, and humans just look at what is and think it is beautiful. But how did humans develop this sense of beauty? How did it evolve? It would seem to have no survival value. Just the opposite – it would seem to distract from the business of survival. What place does the appreciation of beauty have in the dog eat dog world of evolution? It is much more logical to believe that beauty is a gift from a good God.

When we are confronted by scenes of great beauty that thrill our very souls, we know instinctively that such a scene, and our reaction to it, are not just meaningless accidents. Dr. Floyd E. Hamilton in his book *The Basis of Christian Faith*, Harper & Row, New York, 1964, expressed this as follows, at page 43:

The beauty and grandeur of the world arouse feelings of pleasure and appreciation in our souls. A beautiful sunset does not seem like a chance happening. The separation of the different colors of the rainbow through refracted light, the harmony of natural colors, the music of birds, the tinkling and rushing of the waterfall, the majesty of a storm at sea, the bursting of the petals of the rose, the delicate beauty of the African violet, the scent of the English violet – all point to a Cause who planned such things for the enjoyment of mankind and a manifestation of His own glory.

Paul declared to the pagan people of Lystra, people who had no knowledge of the Old Testament Scriptures, that even to them God "has not left Himself without testimony." By looking at the universe around them they could see evidence of God and of His goodness. That is what we have done in this chapter. We have looked at the evidence we can see outside ourselves — evidence from the physical universe — and have seen that the most reasonable explanation of all we see is this — In the beginning God created the heavens and the earth (Gen. 1:1).

Study Questions

1. What is Natural Theism?
2. What evidence do we have that God approves of a study of Natural Theism?
3. Explain the principle of cause and effect.
4. Why must a cause precede and be greater than its effect?
5. Without using the Bible, explain why the universe could not have created itself.
6. Without using the Bible, explain why the universe could not have always existed.
7. Apart from the Bible, what evidence can you give that the universe was created by a supernatural God?
8. Even if the universe evolved from hydrogen gas or cosmic dust, as unbelievers claim, why does this not eliminate the need for a supernatural Designer?
9. Explain why the beauty we see in the world around us is evidence of God.
10. Why are pagan peoples who have never heard of God, still not excused for worshiping idols?

4

NATURAL THEISM, PART TWO

Natural Theism is the science that treats of the existence and character of God in the light of nature and reason. Chapter Three was a study of the evidence we can see outside ourselves, that is evidence we can see in the physical universe around us. Chapter Four will be a study of the evidence we can see within ourselves and of the evidence from human experience.

The Bible declares in Gen.1:27 that God created human beings in His own image. Jesus said, "God is spirit" (John 4:24). If God is spirit, and if humans are created in His image, then humans must also be spiritual beings. This truth is affirmed throughout the Bible. For example: "When Jacob had finished giving instructions to his sons, he drew his feet up into the

BEYOND A REASONABLE DOUBT

bed, breathed his last and was gathered to his people" (Gen. 49:33).

Note that Jacob's body died, but Jacob was gathered to his people. The real person, the spirit, went on living. Or consider these words of Jesus:

> I tell you, my friends, do not be afraid of those who kill the body and after that can do no more. But I will show you whom you should fear: Fear him who, after the killing of the body, has power to throw you into hell. Yes, I tell you, fear him (Luke 12:4-5).

Thus, according to Jesus, the death of the body does not end the existence of a human being, and our real concern should be what happens to us after our bodies are dead. This truth, that humans are spiritual beings, directly conflicts with the atheistic doctrine that nothing exists but physical matter and that the spiritual realm is non-existent. If we can find within ourselves evidence of something more than just physical matter, this becomes evidence for the reality of spiritual things, for the reality of the supernatural, and for the reality of God.

SELF-CONSCIOUSNESS

If physical matter is all that exists, then each of us is nothing but a combination of chemicals come together by chance. But we don't feel like combinations of chemicals, we feel like persons. Each of us feels that the real "me" is something apart from the chemicals that make up the body. We feel that the real person is not physical but spiritual.

We not only live, we can see ourselves living. This

knowledge of ourselves, this self-awareness or self-consciousness, is universal among humans beings and is uniquely human. Other forms of earthly life do not have it because other forms of earthly life are not spiritual beings. Is it possible that all of us are wrong; that we really are not persons, but are only chemicals? Perhaps so, but if we are wrong, then why do we feel the way we do? Why would calcium, carbon, hydrogen, and the other elements that make up our physical bodies have this self-consciousness, this feeling of being a person?

Clearly the humanistic view of man is contrary to the common sense of the whole human race. And just as clearly, a view of man that is contrary to the common sense and innate knowledge of the whole human race, is not apt to be a correct view. Thus, this universal and unique self-consciousness, this awareness of our spiritual nature, is strong evidence that the spirit is real. And if we are spiritual beings, then it follows that there is a spirit world or reality and that there is a supernatural God who also is Spirit.

OUR UNIQUE ABILITY TO REASON

If we are nothing more than the chemicals which compose our bodies, then our thought processes are explained as a "stream of consciousness," each thought feeding on the memories of previous thoughts and flowing on into the thoughts that follow making a continual stream that shifts about as it is affected by external stimuli. It is probable that the thought processes of animals do operate in some way similar to this, and some of our own thoughts when

we day dream, seem to operate similar to this.
But we know that isn't all there is to it. We know
we can control our thoughts. We can direct our brains
to ignore external stimuli and concentrate on some
problem we want to solve. We can change a train of
thought. We can reason about things that have no
connection with our environment. Who is this con-
troller, this director, this changer of direction, this rea-
soner? It is not the chemicals themselves. It is
something apart from the chemicals, it is the real
person — the spirit.

Again our common sense tells us that we are more
than chemicals; that behind our thoughts there is a
thinker; that we are spiritual beings.

OUR MORAL NATURE

If we are nothing but chemicals, then our behavior
is nothing but chemical reactions. The way we act is
determined entirely by the way the chemicals we are
compose of react to the situation we are in. Since
chemicals do not control the way they act, we do not
think of some chemical reactions as moral and some
as immoral. Thus, it makes no sense to condemn
Hitler or Stalin for doing "evil", or to praise Lincoln or
Churchill for doing "good", because there is no good
or evil, only chemical reactions.

But again, our common sense and what we can see
within ourselves tell us this is not true. We know that
some human behavior is good and some is evil. We
know that human behavior is more than chemical
reactions. Thus, we know that human beings are more
than just chemicals.

Even those who claim to believe we are just chemicals do not really live that way – except perhaps in fiction. The leading character in Jack London's famous novel, *The Sea Wolf*, was a brutal sea-captain named Wolf Larson. He was an intelligent, self-educated man who had read the philosophy of atheism and had actually put it to practice. He believed that human life is of no value because all life is nothing but chemicals, a yeasty ferment whose only purpose is to keep squirming a little longer by devouring other life.

At least one atheistic philosopher did carry his philosophy to its logical conclusion. As stated in Chapter Two, the Marquis de Sade did try to live as though he was nothing but chemicals. His brutality toward women kept him in prison or mental institutions for much of his life, and from his name we get our word "sadistic".

Atheistic philosophers can talk like Wolf Larson or the Marquis de Sade. Like the French philosopher, Jean-Paul Sartre, they can say there is no moral difference between helping an old lady across the street, or beating her over the head and snatching her pocketbook. But, after saying this, Sartre signed a manifesto condemning the Algerian War as an "unjust" war. All of us, including atheistic philosophers, are constantly making moral judgments, constantly choosing between right and wrong, just and unjust. Even Wolf Larson found some right or purpose in life – the purpose to go on living. Why would chemicals have such a desire as that?

Human beings do have a moral sense or conscience. It is real and it is powerful. A guilty conscience is the most destructive of all human emotions. It is so powerful that it can ruin a person's life, destroy health, and drive to an early grave. Our conscience is not an infallible guide to what is right, but it is a powerful force that tells us we ought to do what we believe to be right. It is possessed by no other form of earthly life. It certainly is not possessed by chemicals.

Our moral sense or conscience is not an instinct. It may tell us how we ought to choose between instincts — whether we should obey the herd instinct to rush into a burning house to save a child's life, or obey the survival instinct and stay away from the fire. Our moral sense is not something that evolved. More often than not it lacks survival value. When the Miranda case was decided, requiring that persons under arrest be advised that they do not have to answer any questions and if they do their answers can be used against them in court, it was generally believed this would almost end the use of confessions in criminal cases. But that has not been true, for many defendants still confess, driven by their sense of guilt, even though they know the confession will be used against them.

This moral sense, this powerful force within us that urges us to do what we believe to be right, tells us that we are more than just chemicals. We are spiritual beings with a moral nature given to us by a moral Creator. This, together with other attributes that we can see within ourselves, our self-consciousness and our unique ability to reason, cannot be explained by chemicals alone. They are convincing evidence of our spiritual nature, and thus evidence of the realness of the spirit world and of the supernatural God.

OUR POWER OF CHOICE

Harvard University's famous professor of psychology, B. F. Skinner, believed that both the human spirit and God are superstitions that originated in man's inability to understand his world. He taught that freedom and free will are no more than illusions and that man is completely controlled by external influences. Because he could condition rats and pigeons to always react in a certain way, he was certain that human behavior can be predicted and shaped exactly as if it were a chemical reaction.

Of course, if the humanistic view of man is correct, then Dr. Skinner was correct. If we are just chemicals, nothing more, then our behavior must be just chemical reactions, nothing more. And if this is so, then once we learn enough about chemicals, we can predict exactly what any person will do under any given set of circumstances. Thus, we are not "persons" at all, but are nothing more than complicated machines.

Directly opposed to this is the Christian view of man. Basic to the whole Bible message is the truth that human beings do possess a free will. Humans do have the power to choose and they are responsible for the choices they make. Courageous old Joshua challenged the Israelites to take a stand, as follows:

> Now fear the LORD and serve him with all faithfulness. Throw away the gods your forefathers worshiped beyond the River and in Egypt, and serve the LORD. But if serving the LORD seems undesirable to you, then choose for yourselves this day whom you will serve, whether the gods your forefathers served beyond the River, or the gods of the Amorites, in whose land you are living. But as for me and my household, we will serve the LORD (Josh. 24:14-15).

Again it is obvious that the humanistic view of man as a chemical machine is contrary to what we see and experience every day. We are constantly making

59

choices and we see others doing the same. We know that we can think, and decide, and choose to do one thing or do just the opposite. Our common sense and daily experience tell us that this power to choose is real. It does not come from chemicals because chemicals do not make choices. It can come only from the person within — from the spirit. It is proof that we are more than chemicals, and thus proof that the spiritual world is real.

HUMAN EXPERIENCES OF A SPIRITUAL NATURE

Secular humanists claim that nothing exists but physical matter/energy, and thus that human beings are nothing but chance combinations of chemicals. If this is true, then every human experience can be explained according to the natural laws that apply to those chemicals. But if, as Christians claim, humans are spiritual beings, then it is possible for them to have experiences of a spiritual nature — experiences that cannot be explained by natural laws, but require supernatural explanations. Thus, the important question to be considered here is — do human beings ever have experiences which cannot be explained by the laws of nature?

Throughout history, thousands of people have reported experiencing miracles, providential happenings, and answered prayers. No doubt many of these were coincidence, many were mistakes, many were falsehoods. But it is not necessary that we prove all of them. In fact, if just one of these actually occurred, then we know that something exists other than physical matter. If any of these reports were made by persons of high integrity and sound judgment, who actually witnessed the event, and were able to correctly evaluate what they saw, then such testimony is good, admissible, evidence of the spiritual nature of human beings, and of the reality of supernatural events. It becomes one more converging line of evidence, pointing to the reality of the spirit world, to the reality of supernatural events, and to the existence of God.

A MIRACULOUS ANSWER TO PRAYER

Boyce Mouton has written a book published by College Press, Joplin, Missouri, entitled *Beyond the Veil,* in which he has collected a number of reports of miracles and providential happenings. These reports have been carefully selected and come only from persons of unquestioned integrity. They amply demonstrate the reality of supernatural intervention in human affairs. The following example is from pages 106·and 107:

> Dr. Garland Bare is quoted several times in this book. His name is synonymous with integrity to all who know him. He has lived a life of faith and can tell stories by the hour about answers to prayer.
>
> Among the most remarkable experiences of his life was a miraculous healing which took place in Pua, Thailand in 1973.
>
> A young man named Ban Chong wanted to become a Christian. His father was a witch-doctor and forbade him to do so. In order to keep him away from the influence of the missionaries Ban Chong was banished to the mountains for a year to care for the cattle. Here he was stricken with falciparum malaria and was brought to the hospital where Dr. Bare was practicing.
>
> For some forty eight hours Dr. Bare used every new medical treatment and technique available, but to no

avail. Ban Chong only became worse.

Finally, as a last resort, they began dripping quinine into his veins. At this point the patient began to hemorrhage in his digestive tract and bladder. The condition was described as "black water fever" as it causes the urine to turn black.

Dr. Bare then gave Ban Chong a transfusion. In that remote area only one suitable donor could be found and he weighed but 90 pounds. One unit of blood was given but it did no good.

By now Ban Chong's blood pressure was 80/20. His family was summoned to his bedside and informed that he was dying. His witch-doctor father came with his brother, Jur Sha, who was a Christian elder.

Father — "Can God heal my son?"

Dr. Bare — "God can do all things!"

Father — "If he becomes a Christian will that guarantee his healing?"

Dr. Bare — "No!"

Father — "One year ago I forbade him to become a Christian, but now I am willing if he wants to."

Ban Chong — It is too late — I am dying."

Dr. Bare — ."You can give what is left of your life to God."

Ban Chong — "I can't pray — I have on the spirit strings."

(Spirit strings are articles associated with demon worship. By now Ban Chong's blood pressure was 50/0 — his extremities were cold and his eyes were glazed. Dr. Bare asked for scissors and removed the spirit strings.)

Ban Chong — "God, I am dying. If it is at all possible save me!"

At this point Dr. Bare said that immediately Ban Chong's color returned to his face and his bloated stomach became flat. Dr. Bare asked for a blood pressure reading and the nurse said it was 120/70. His pulse was 80 and regular and he had no more fever or other symptoms of malaria.

Since it was late Friday night Ban Chong remained

in the hospital until morning and then was released a well man. On Sunday he was baptized into Christ along with his father and other members of the family.

Healing such as this can only be explained as the supernatural intervention of God. Actually such healings occur with great frequency. Nearly everyone knows of healings that defy medical explanation. Perhaps some are the result of some natural cause. But it is not reasonable to insist that all can be explained away on natural grounds.

A PROVIDENTIAL ANSWER TO PRAYER

At page 39 of *Beyond the Veil*, Boyce Mouton recorded an incident that was reported to him by Roy Weece. Mr. Weece served the church at Eldon, Missouri, for many years and, for about 20 years, has been a campus minister at the University of Missouri at Columbia. He is one of the best known preachers in America, and thousands could testify to his integrity and sound judgment. Therefore, the following quote from Mr. Weece's eyewitness account would be accepted by any jury as truthful evidence.

Several years ago I became convinced on the basis of John 7:17 that God does give subjective evidence to the believer. This evidence will not contradict objective or revealed truth, nor will it precede our obedience to God. There must be obedience and trust in my life for this subjective evidence to occur.

Acts 8 was also intriguing to me. Philip, the Christian, was directed to the Ethiopian nobleman to tell him about Jesus and baptize him along the road. I figured that if God could lead people together in that day, I couldn't see any reason why He couldn't lead people together in this day. So I decided to pray that God would guide me to people.

One example of this guidance came out west of Eldon, Missouri, in the vicinity of Versailles. I had been given the name of a man who lived in that vicinity. I had been told that he worked during the daytime and that I would have to catch him in the evening, but still I felt a strong compulsion to go down that road, and go into his yard. I had never been there before. I came up to his porch and knocked on the door and just about turned to walk away, for I just knew that he wouldn't be there.

Then the door opened, and there he stood. I introduced myself and said that I was a Christian and that I wanted to talk with him. He said, "Come right in." He took me over to a chair. On the chair was a gun. He said, "I was just seated on this chair with this gun to my temple. I had decided that life was not worth going on. Then I decided that before I did it I would try to call on God. And so I laid the gun aside, knelt down at this chair, and said, God, send somebody to help me."

It was at that moment that Roy Weece knocked on the door. Could this have been a remarkable coincidence? Was it just chance that Roy Weece felt a compulsion to drive to a house, where he fully expected to find no one at home, and to arrive just as the man inside, on the verge of suicide, had knelt to ask God to send someone to help him? The odds against such a sequence of events are astronomical. Certainly this is relevant, reliable, evidence that the things of the spirit are real. Add to the two examples presented here, countless other reports of a similar nature, and this becomes a strong line of evidence pointing to the truth of the Christian view of reality.

OTHER SPIRITUAL EXPERIENCES

So far, we have considered spiritual experiences that involve the action or intervention of God — miracles, providential happenings, and answered prayers. There is good evidence that human beings have other experiences of a non-material nature, usually referred to as "psychic phenomena". Included in this category are:

Extra-sensory perception (ESP) — Perception that is outside the realm of the senses.

Telepathy — Communication between minds by some means other than normal sensory channels.

Clairvoyance — The ability to perceive things that cannot be seen.

Premonition — A forewarning received by some means other than the normal sensory channels.

Psycho-kinesis — Moving objects by some non-physical means.

Obviously these phenomena, if they really happen, disprove the basic belief of atheism — that nothing exists but physical matter and that everything operates according to natural laws. For this reason, most scientists, although supposedly engaged in an objective search for the truth, have ignored the evidence for psychic phenomena and comparatively little research has been done in this field.

Sir Alister Hardy, formerly head of the zoology department at Oxford University, and knighted for his outstanding work in biological research, in a book entitled, *The Living Stream* (Harper & Row, New York, 1965) made this statement, page 285;

If only 1 per cent of the money spent upon the physical and biological sciences could be spent upon investigations of religious experience and upon psychical research, it might not be long before a new age of faith dawned upon the world.

At page 235, Sir Alister Hardy included this quote taken from his Presidential Address to the Zoology Section of the British Association in 1949;

> There is another matter which I feel it only right to mention if one is not to be intellectually dishonest. There has appeared over the horizon something which many of us do not like to look at. If it is pointed out to us we say: "No, it can't be there, our doctrines say it is impossible." I refer to telepathy – the communication of one mind with another by means other than by the ordinary senses. I believe that no one, who examines the evidence with an unbiased mind, can reject it.

What is this "something which many of us do not like to look at"; this dreaded knowledge that causes scientists to abandon their claim to be open-minded searchers for truth? It is evidence that the spirit world is real, that the God they have ignored is there, and that the judgment they hoped to escape lies ahead. But despite this bias, this unscientific refusal even to consider the possibility of such things, some scientific research into psychic phenomena has been done, most notably at Duke University by Professor Rhine and others. This research has provided unassailable statistical proof of the reality of telepathy, clairvoyance, and psycho-kinesis. Quoting Dr. Matthews, the Dean of St. Paul's, in his Maurice Lectures, published by the Oxford University Press in 1950, "The case for telepathy is so strong that one is tempted to say that

NATURAL THEISM, PART TWO

the only way to retain disbelief in it is by steadily ignoring the evidence."

What does all this mean? What does the reality of these so-called "psychic phenomena" do to the basic beliefs of atheism? At page 238 of his book, Sir Alister Hardy quoted Professor H.H. Price, then Wykeham Professor of Logic at Oxford, as follows:

> Telepathy is something which ought not to happen at all, if the Materialistic theory were true. But it does happen. So there must be something seriously wrong with the Materialistic theory, however numerous and imposing the normal facts which support it may be.

Many people doubt the reality of these so-called "psychic phenomena". However, as seen above, they have been confirmed by some scientific studies, and they are accepted by some highly reputable scientists and scholars. Thus, while the case for Christianity certainly does not depend on psychic phenomena, this is one more line of evidence indicating that human beings are more than just chemicals, and that the universe contains more than just physical matter.

THE UNIVERSAL DESIRE FOR GOD

All over the world, even in the most remote places and among the most primitive peoples, there is belief in the spirit world, belief in supernatural events, and belief in some sort of deity. Atheists claim this universal belief is the result of man's need to explain death, and they have made charts purporting to show how religion evolved from animism through polytheism, on up to monotheism and, finally, to humanism (God is dead).

67

Such charts are based on little but wishful thinking. The actual evidence from archaeology and anthropology indicates that all around the world the original concept was of one God who was the Creator, and that this original knowledge was gradually lost and degenerated into the paganism of later times. Sir Alister Hardy in his book cited above, page 272, quotes from E. Evans-Pritchard, then Professor of Social Anthropology at Oxford, as follows:

> The theories of writers about primitive religion have not been sustained by research. During the last century what was presented as theory was generally the supposition that some particular form of religion was the most primitive and that from it developed other forms, the development being sometimes presented as a succession of inevitable and well-defined stages. . . . All this was for the most part pure conjecture."

If human beings are nothing but accidental combinations of chemicals, where did this idea of God and this desire for God come from? Why would carbon, hydrogen, iron, and the other chemical elements that compose the human body, long for a creator? Certainly this is more evidence that we are spiritual beings, created by a supernatural God who is also Spirit, and who placed in us a desire for Him.

Study Questions

1. Explain why the Christian belief that humans are spiritual beings is in direct conflict with the doctrines of atheism.

2. What is self-consciousness? What does this tell you about yourself?

3. Explain why your thought processes are more than just chemical reactions.

4. What does our moral nature tell us about the reality of the spirit world?

5. Explain why your moral sense or conscience is not an instinct.

6. Why are our self-consciousness, our ability to reason, and our moral sense all evidence for the existence of God?

7. Why is it unreasonable to reject all reports of miracles and providential happenings as being untrue because they are impossible?

8. Why have many scientists been reluctant to investigate such things as telepathy and clairvoyance?

9. Why are even such evil practices as witchcraft evidence against atheism?

10.Why is the universal desire for God evidence that God does exist?

5

EVIDENCE FOR THE OTHER SIDE

In chapters three and four we have considered 10 separate lines of evidence, all of which point to the truth of these facts: that God does exist; that the spirit world is real; and that supernatural events do occur. All of this evidence is separate and apart from the Bible. It is evidence we can see in the universe around us, evidence we can see within ourselves, and evidence we can observe from human experience. Chapters eight through thirteen will present evidence for the truth of Christianity — evidence for the inspiration of the Bible and for the deity of Christ. Of course, that evidence will also be further proof of the existence of God, of the spirit world, and of supernatural events. But the 10 lines of evidence we have considered this far are:

1. Evidence from cause and effect.
2. Evidence from design.
3. Evidence from beauty.
4. Evidence from human self-consciousness.
5. Evidence from the human ability to reason.
6. Evidence from the human moral nature.
7. Evidence from the human ability to choose.
8. Evidence from reports of miracles, providential happenings, and answered prayers.
9. Evidence from other spiritual experiences.
10. Evidence from the universal desire for God.

These 10 converging lines of evidence are proof beyond a reasonable doubt of God's existence and of the reality of spiritual things and supernatural events, and would easily satisfy the standards of proof set by a court of law, unless other evidence was offered that disproves or explains away the affirmative evidence. Since Christianity claims to be the religion of truth and knowledge, it is certainly fair and appropriate that we consider the evidence for the other side. That is the purpose of chapters five, six, and seven.

GOD AND THE SPIRIT WORLD CANNOT BE SEEN

The first Russian astronaut into space said he looked all around and did not see God, implying that this confirmed his atheism. Of course, the fact that God and spirits are not visible to us, is not proof that they do not exist, and probably few atheists would claim it is. We cannot see gravity either, but we believe that it exists because we can see its results. In like manner, we can see the results of God — evidence of what He

72

has done and is doing – and thus believe He exists. That God is invisible actually strengthens our faith and confidence in Him, because we can see that all visible things are wasting away.

> So we fix our eyes not on what is seen, but on what is unseen. For what is seen is temporary, but what is unseen is eternal (II Cor. 4:18).

MAN IS TOO INSIGNIFICANT FOR GOD TO CARE ABOUT

The late Harlow Shapley, world famous astronomer at Harvard University, in a speech delivered some years ago at Carthage, Missouri, explained how insignificant the earth is in the enormous universe, and then suggested that, if there is a God out there, human beings are very egotistical to believe that a God with so much to look after could have time for them.

This argument, however, is based on the same anthropomorphism (attributing human characteristics to God) that is exhibited by the most primitive pagan religions, and of which unbelievers often accuse the Bible. One of the favorite attacks on the Bible is that the writers have fabricated a god in the image of man. It is true that man was created in the image of God, and thus, man has some attributes in common with God. But the Bible never teaches that man is equal to God and never attributes to God the imperfections and limitations of men – in fact, just the opposite:

> For my thoughts are not your thoughts, neither are your ways my ways," declares the LORD. As the

73

heavens are higher than the earth, so are my ways higher than your ways and my thoughts than your thoughts (Isa. 55:8-9).

So it is surprising that modern scientists and scholars should fall into the primitive error of anthropomorphism by making this argument. Certainly the all knowing, all powerful, ever present, supernatural God who created the universe is not limited by the size of His own creation. He can mark the fall of every sparrow and number the hairs of every head. The inability of modern scientists to understand how God can do all this is more evidence of His supernatural greatness.

THE PROBLEM OF SUFFERING

If God exists, and He is good, and He is all powerful, then why is there so much suffering in the world? Unbelievers argue that either God is not good, or He is not all powerful, or He does not exist. Not only is this a favorite argument of unbelievers, the problem of suffering also is troubling to many Christians. We cannot expect to know all of the answers from our limited human knowledge, but the following suggestions do throw some light on the problem and are enough to show that the presence of suffering in the world is not convincing evidence that God does not exist, or that He is not good and all powerful.

1. Can we know joy without sorrow, pleasure without pain? Perhaps we need the suffering of this life before we can appreciate the full joy of heaven.

2. We are not robots. God gave us free will — the power to choose. This freedom carries with it the possibility of our doing evil and causing suffering. Much

suffering results from man's sin.

3. Our sense of values is often wrong because we lack the perspective of eternity. The things we value most, money, long life, good health, physical beauty, athletic ability, may be of comparatively small value, or may even be harmful to us.

4. Suffering may be beneficial to the sufferer. The Apostle Paul suffered from a thorn in the flesh that, by teaching him humility and making him more dependent upon God, actually made him into a better preacher. Great musicians and writers are sometimes those who have suffered. Suffering can teach discipline and cause the sufferer to focus his life upon those things that really count. Most important of all, suffering can lead one to God and thus bestow eternal blessings.

5. Suffering may produce good for others. A child with leukemia, a family left destitute by fire, a city devastated by an earthquake, all these bring an outpouring of love and generosity that demonstrates the very best in people, and we can only guess at the eternal good that results. The courage of those who suffer sometimes inspires others to greater heights. And, as Tiny Tim pointed out, suffering can make others more grateful to God for the blessings they have.

6. Some suffering may be a warning of judgment to come. As such, it is really a great kindness from God.

7. Some suffering is deserved as just punishment for sin. An arrogant creature that defies, ridicules, and disobeys its own Creator actually deserves more punishment than ever received in this life.

8. The Christian faith is not a religion of comfort and ease that would produce moral and cultural decay for mankind. We are not promised freedom from

suffering, but the spiritual power to overcome suffering.

9. Finally, and most importantly, if the evidence proves that God exists and is our Creator, then we have no right to question anything He does. The clay does not say to the Potter, "Why have you made me thus?" If He is the Creator of the universe, then His wisdom so far surpasses ours that it is the height of arrogance for us to tell Him what is right and wrong, or how He should run the universe.

We need to trust God enough to know that, whether we understand it or not, He can always bring good out of evil. Remember, the greatest evil the world has seen was the crucifixion of Jesus Christ. Yet from that tragedy, God brought forth the greatest good the world has seen.

A world without sorrow, without pain, without failure, would also be a world without joy, without pleasure, without success. It would be dull and monotonous, a robot-like existence that would rob us of our humanity. Even with our limited knowledge we can see that suffering in the world is not proof that God does not exist, nor is it proof that He lacks goodness and power.

THE SUPPOSED GREAT AGE OF THE EARTH

That the earth is billions of years old is an essential doctrine of atheism, and is probably considered by atheists to be their strongest argument against Christianity. In their debates with creationists, evolutionists always dwell on this age question. Actually, the age of the earth is a separate question from evolution versus creation, but it is related, because, while creation could have occurred whether the earth is young or old, evolution must have a very old earth. So the age of the earth question is vital to evolution. An old earth does not prove that evolution did happen, but a young earth does prove it did not happen.

The age of the earth, also, is a separate question from the existence or non-existence of God and the spirit world. God can exist regardless of the age of the earth. But the age question is the favorite point of attack against the Bible and has been used to undermine the faith of many in God and in the reality of things spiritual and supernatural.

Christians have resorted to various means of reconciling the Bible to the supposed great age of the earth. One such means is to treat the Genesis days as geologic ages during which God created by means of evolution. This is sometimes called theistic evolution. Of course, this is not impossible. God could have created by any method He chose. But this theory does place a strained construction upon the language of the Bible. Also, evolution would seem to be a clumsy and inefficient way for God to go about the work of creation. And finally, if God did create by evolution, the evidence should appear in the fossil record. As will be seen later, the evidence is not there.

Others have suggested that the Genesis days were short periods of creative activity, separated by long ages without any creation going on. The sedimentary rocks, fossils, and other appearances of great age, are assigned to the intervening ages. This theory rejects evolution and thus avoids the problems connected with it. However, while it is not impossible, this theory also puts a strained construction upon the language of the Bible.

Probably the most popular means of reconciling the Bible to the supposed great age of the earth, is the gap theory. This theory accepts the 6 days of creation described in Genesis, Chapter One, as being 6 consecutive 24 hour days and agrees they occurred about 6000 years ago. However, the first day began with Genesis 1:3. The creation of the heavens and the earth, as described in Genesis 1:1, occurred some time before that. All we are told is that it was "In the beginning," which could have been a few years or even billions of years before the 6 days of creative activity. Since the word "was" in Genesis 1:2 can also be translated "became", this theory holds that the 2nd verse tells us of the destruction of all that was on the earth previous to the 6 day creation period, so that "the earth became formless and empty," and that sometime thereafter, God created in 6 days the things we see now.

According to this gap theory, we are not told what was on the earth prior to its becoming formless and empty, because those things have nothing to do with the story of redemption, which is the main theme of the Bible. For all we know, the earth could have been teaming with plant and animal life back at that time, and this could explain fossils, coal beds, oil deposits, etc. Again it must be said that this theory is possible, and it is accepted by some sincere, Bible-believing Christians. But many others believe that the gap theory requires a strained construction of the Bible and thus reject it.

Treating the Genesis days as actual 24 hour days following immediately one after another, best fits the language of the Bible, and probably is accepted by most conservative Christians, although not all accept the 6000 year age suggested by Ussher's chronology. The genealogies listed in Genesis, Chapters 5 and 11 may not include all of the links, as Moses may have eliminated some of the less important men for the sake of brevity. But even if this is true, it still leaves a young age for the earth, so the question remains — can an intelligent person look at the available evidence and still reasonably believe in an earth age measured in thousands of years instead of billions of years? For the following reasons, the answer to that question is yes:

1. Creation necessarily involves the appearance of age. Adam was created a grown man. When he was only 10 seconds old, an anthropologist may have estimated his age at 21 years. If plants were to be created, it may have been necessary to create soil to sustain the plants and, also, to create a process to continually replenish the soil. But a geologist looking at this soil and the replenishing process only seconds after the creation, would have calculated a great age for the earth based on the amount of soil he found. No matter what is created, that is, brought into existence from non-existence, it will immediately appear to be older than it actually is. To deny this is to deny the possibility of creation, which, as we have seen before, is unreasonable to do.

Therefore, everything we see on the earth, regardless of how old it may appear, could have been created by God in a moments time and put here for our use or for some other purpose of His own. Does this make God a deceiver? Certainly not, because He tells us in His Word what was done, and we are deceived only if we choose to disregard what He has said.

2. The various dating methods used by scientists to compute a great age for the earth require at least two assumptions, neither of which can be shown to be true. First, they must assume what the condition of the material was when the process began, and second, they must assume that the process itself has always proceeded at the same rate throughout elapsed time. Not only are scientists unable to show the validity of these assumptions, there is growing evidence from geology that mountains were raised, canyons were cut, rock strata were deposited, and fossils were buried, not by gradual, uniform processes, but by sudden catastrophes.

The old idea of uniformitarianism, which geologists have believed so long, and upon which Darwin relied so heavily, is giving way to catastrophism. Since it is now clear that conditions have not continued in a uniform manner, it is no longer reasonable to believe that the timing processes are accurate.

3. There are many dating methods which show a very young age for the earth. An excellent book by Dr. Henry M. Morris and Dr. Gary E. Parker, entitled *What is Creation Science*, Master Books, El Cajon, Calif., 1987, contains a list of 68 dating methods which vary in indicated age for the earth from 500 million years down to 100 years. Of course none of these processes is really accurate because of the assumptions that must be made and because of the influence of outside factors. Nevertheless, the fact that many scientists rely on those processes that indicate the earth is very old while ignoring those processes that point to a young age, is revealing evidence of unscientific bias.

4. Actually most of the dating is based on the assumption that evolution is true. Rock strata are

dated by the fossils they contain, and since, according to evolution, the fossils are very old, it follows that the rocks are also very old. But, as will be seen in chapters six and seven, the overwhelming weight of scientific evidence is against evolution. Of course, if evolution is not true, neither are the dates given for the rocks.

In books, in museums, in schools, in the news media, we are constantly confronted by the assumption of a great age for the earth. Christians should remember that this is just an assumption. In addition to the evidence against a great age that is presented in this chapter, chapters eight and nine will present evidence for the truth and inspiration of the Bible, and that will be the best evidence of all that God created the heavens and the earth, and that He did it when the Bible says He did.

CHRISTIANITY ONLY ONE OF MANY RELIGIONS

It is claimed that the Bible is only one of many great religious books, and that Christianity is only one of several great religions. Since these other religions also have large followings, it is argued that they should be treated as equal to Christianity. Furthermore, it is argued that the proliferation of hundreds of cults, many of them offshoots from Christianity, shows that all religion is man-made and unreliable.

None of the foregoing should surprise a Christian. Jesus made it very clear that most people would not follow Him:

> Enter through the narrow gate. For wide is the gate and broad is the road that leads to destruction, and many enter through it. But small is the gate and

narrow the road that leads to life, and only a few find it (Matt. 7:13-14).

The apostles repeatedly warned that false teachers would arise, and that many would follow them, even many Christians:

> But there were also false prophets among the people, just as there will be false teachers among you. They will secretly introduce destructive heresies, even denying the sovereign Lord who bought them—bringing swift destruction on themselves. Many will follow their shameful ways and will bring the way of truth into disrepute. In their greed these teachers will exploit you with stories they have made up. Their condemnation has long been hanging over them, and their destruction has not been sleeping (II Pet. 2:1-3).

Note what an amazing prophecy this is. Peter stated that false teachers would arise among the Christians, that many would follow them, that they would bring the way of truth into disrepute, that they would be greedy, and that they would exploit their followers with stories they have made up. How often we have seen this prophecy fulfilled in our own time, and how we have marveled to see seemingly intelligent people exploited by obvious frauds. Instead of being an argument against Christianity, the exact fulfillment of such prophecy is convincing evidence in its favor.

Furthermore, a study of the causes of the growth of the other great world religions shows that their growth can be explained by natural causes — by military force; by political and social pressure; by appealing to the lower nature of mankind; by demanding little or no moral regeneration; by the use of ritualism; and by compromise with other religions. On the other hand, the early growth of Christianity cannot be explained by natural causes, although in later years some corrupted forms of Christianity did grow in this way.

The early Christian Church grew rapidly in spite of the following adverse factors:

1. It was not spread by force or political power. In fact, Christians were cruelly persecuted and oppressed.

2. It was not spread by social pressure or influence. In fact, Christians were looked down upon and often became outcasts, even from their own families.

3. It was not spread by economic advantage. In fact, Christians often lost their jobs, had their property confiscated, and became poor and destitute.

4. It was not spread by promising salvation through ritualism. In fact, Christians were told that physical rites would not save them.

5. It was not spread by appealing to man's lower nature. In fact, it demanded a drastic change in the way people lived.

6. It was not spread by compromise with other religions. In fact, it claimed to be the only true religion and refused to submit to Greek paganism or even to obey the Roman demand to worship the emperor.

The amazing growth of the early Christian Church, despite all these powerful forces working against it, cannot be explained on natural grounds. Such growth is strong evidence that the Church was from God, was guided by the Holy Spirit, and was blessed with supernatural gifts. The wise Jewish teacher, Gamaliel, correctly assessed the prospects for the new Christian Church, as follows:

> Therefore, in the present case I advise you: Leave these men alone! Let them go! For if their purpose or activity is of human origin, it will fail. But if it is from

God, you will not be able to stop these men; you will only find yourselves fighting against God (Acts 5:38-39).

Actually none of these 5 arguments offers any real evidence that God does not exist or that Christianity is not true. Instead they are merely assertions by man that God should have done things differently. In his arrogance, man offers advice to God. You should not be invisible. You should not have made the universe so large. You should not permit bad things to happen to people. You should not allow people to choose other religions. You cannot just create a canyon or a valley, or scour one out with a great flood, but instead you must start with a plateau and let the water and wind gradually cut out the canyons and the valleys.

God answered this kind of foolish arrogance many centuries ago:

Then the LORD answered Job out of the storm. He said: "Who is this that darkens my counsel with words without knowledge? Brace yourself like a man; I will question you, and you shall answer me. Where were you when I laid the earth's foundation? Tell me, if you understand. Who marked off its dimensions? Surely you know! Who stretched a measuring line across it? On what were its footings set, or who laid its cornerstone— (Job 38:1-6).

Study Questions

1. Why should Christians never fear the truth?

2. What is anthropomorphism? Explain how unbelieving scientists are sometimes guilty of this.

3. How is the problem of suffering used as an argu-

ment against God?

4. Give at least 4 reasons why God may permit suffering.

5. Why is a great age for the earth a vital doctrine of atheism?

6. What are some of the ways that some Christians have attempted to reconcile the Bible to the supposed great age of the earth?

7. Explain why it is reasonable for an intelligent Christian to believe the earth is comparatively young.

8. Why is the fact that so many people follow false teachers and bizarre cults, actually proof of the existence of God and the truth of the Bible?

9. Why is the rapid growth of the early Christian Church evidence that it was from God?

10. What caused the growth of the other great religions of the world?

6

EVOLUTION, PART ONE

The ten lines of evidence presented in chapters three and four are easily sufficient to prove, even apart from the Bible, that God exists, and that the spirit world is real, and that supernatural events do occur — unless evidence can be produced by the other side to undermine or disprove the affirmative evidence. In chapter five, we considered five lines of evidence that have been used by the other side, and demonstrated that none of them disproves the existence of God, or spiritual things, or supernatural events. None of the evidence in chapter five in any way undermines the evidence in chapters three and four.

In chapters six and seven, we continue with the

examination of the evidence for the other side. These two chapters deal with the most important doctrine of humanism — the theory of evolution. There are just two ways to explain the existence of the universe — creation or evolution. If the universe were created, then a supernatural Creator is necessary, and thus, there can be no doubt that God does exist, that He dwells in the spirit world, and that He can do supernatural things.

Furthermore, if God is the Creator, then He owns everything in the universe, including human beings; He has the right to demand our obedience; and He can punish us for our disobedience. Thus the whole secular humanistic faith depends upon evolution. It is the only way to escape from God. This explains why unbelieving scientists cling so desperately to evolution, despite the growing mountain of evidence against it, and it explains why secular humanists fight so vigorously to suppress any mention of creation science in our public schools, or in any of our public discourse.

BOTH CREATION AND EVOLUTION ARE MATTERS OF FAITH

The claim is often made that evolution is a proven scientific fact. That claim is not true. Scientific fact or law is established by observation or by re-enactment and by repeated testing. No human was present to observe either creation or evolution, and no human can re-enact either creation or evolution. Thus, neither creation nor evolution can ever be established as a scientific law. Both must remain matters of faith.

Reference is made in Chapter 2 to a recent book entitled *Darwin on Trial* by Phillip Johnson. Professor Johnson is a graduate of Harvard and the University of Chicago and served as a law clerk for Chief Justice Earl Warren of the United States Supreme Court. He has taught law for over 20 years at the University of California at Berkeley. His excellent book testifies to his expertness in matters of logic and evidence. His educational and professional background makes any bias in favor of conservatism very unlikely. In fact, he describes himself as a philosophical theist and a Christian who believes that God could have created out of nothing or could have used some evolutionary process.

He took up the study of Darwinism because he saw that the books defending the theory were dogmatic and unconvincing. His carefully reasoned conclusion is that Darwinism has become a stubbornly uncompromising and emotionally defended religious faith. The following quotation is from page 9:

> Another factor that makes evolutionary science seem a lot like religion is the evident zeal of Darwinists to evangelize the world, by insisting that even non-scientists accept the truth of their theory as a matter of moral obligation. Richard Dawkins, an Oxford zoologist who is one of the most influential figures in evolutionary science, is unabashedly explicit about the religious side of Darwinism. His 1986 book *The Blind Watchmaker* is at one level about biology, but at a more fundamental level it is a sustained argument for atheism. According to Dawkins, "Darwin made it possible to be an intellectually fulfilled atheist."
>
> When he contemplates the perfidy of those who refuse to believe, Dawkins can scarcely restrain his fury. "It is absolutely safe to say that, if you meet somebody who claims not to believe in evolution, that

person is ignorant, stupid or insane (or wicked, but I'd rather not consider that)." Dawkins went on to explain, by the way, that what he dislikes particularly about creationists is that they are intolerant.

The fact that creation and evolution are both matters of faith rather than scientific law, does not mean they are not subject to scientific investigation or that we are unable to arrive at any sound conclusions concerning them. We can still look at the evidence to see which is a reasonable faith, and which is unreasonable. We can look at the results, at what we can see and learn about the universe today, and determine which theory most reasonably and accurately explains those results. Chapters six and seven are a study of the results — the evidence that has been found and the scientific facts that have been proven — to see which way the evidence points — toward evolution or toward creation.

The trial of a case in a court of law sometimes involves evidence of a scientific or technical nature. In such cases, expert witnesses are called to assist the jury in understanding the evidence. In evaluating the testimony of an expert witness it is very important to know his qualifications and to know if he is subject to any bias or prejudice. Following is a list of the experts who will be quoted in chapters six and seven, along with their qualifications and grounds for possible bias.

SIR ALISTER HARDY was born in England, graduated from Oxford University, and after teaching at the University of Hull and the University of Aberdeen, he became head of the Department of Zoology at Oxford University. He was elected a Fellow of the Royal Society in 1940 and was knighted in 1957. His book quoted here is *The Living Stream*, Harper and Row,

1965. He was an evolutionist but was troubled by problems which he felt evolution could not explain by natural laws alone. He remained an evolutionist but concluded that evolution must be guided by some unknown spiritual force.

SIR FRED HOYLE is also an Englishman, a professor at Cambridge University. He founded the Cambridge Institute of Theoretical Astronomy in 1967. He was made a Fellow of the Royal Society in 1957 and was elected as associate member of the American National Academy of Sciences in 1969 — the highest U. S. honor for non-American scientists. He was knighted in 1972, and in 1974 was awarded a Royal Medal by the Queen in recognition of his contribution to theoretical physics and cosmology. His book quoted here is *The Intelligent Universe*, Holt, Rinehart and Winston, 1983. He is an evolutionist but believes that Darwinism and its modern modifications are plainly wrong. He argues that life is far too complex to have risen by random processes, but that evolution was directed by some intelligence in outer space that sent the components of life to earth on cosmic particles.

MICHAEL DENTON is an Australian medical doctor and molecular biologist. He is currently doing biological research in Sidney. His book quoted here is *Evolution: A Theory in Crisis*, Adler & Adler, 1986. He is an evolutionist but believes that Darwinism and its modern modifications are on extremely shaky ground. He points out many serious problems with evolution including the fact that modern molecular biology has cast serious doubt on the theory. He is unwilling to accept creation, and instead, seems to be waiting for some other explanation of origins.

HENRY M. MORRIS received his B.S. from Rice University and his M.S. and Ph.D. from the University of Minnesota with a major in hydraulics and hydrology and minors in geology and mathematics. He spent 28 years on the faculties of 5 universities, 18 of those years as chairman of academic departments. He was formerly an evolutionist but switched to creationism and is presently President of the Institute for Creation Research. His book quoted here is *What Is Creation Science?* Master Books, 1987, which he wrote together with Dr. Gary E. Parker.

GARY E. PARKER earned his doctorate in biology, with a cognate in geology (paleontology). He is the author of four programmed textbooks in biology and was elected to the American Society of Zoologists. He taught biology at the college level for 10 years, first as an evolutionist. After switching to creationism, he became Chairman of the Biology Department at Christian Heritage College.

From the foregoing, it should be clear that the experts to be quoted are extremely well qualified and are more likely to be biased in favor of evolution than creation. The books described above may be referred to merely by the author's last name and the page numbers.

THE FIRST LAW OF THERMODYNAMICS

Morris and Parker at page 201:

The First Law of Thermodynamics (also known as the Law of Conservation of Energy — which in our nuclear age, is known also to include Mass or Matter) states that there can be no creation or annihilation of Mass/Energy. One form of Energy can be converted into another, one state of Matter can be converted into another, and there can even be Matter/Energy inter-conversions, but the totality of Mass/Energy in the universe remains constant. The Two Laws of Thermodynamics are the most universal and best-proved laws which science has . . .

Evolution requires a natural process for bringing matter into existence. This implies a natural process for taking matter out of existence. Yet by every observation that scientists have ever made and by every experiment that scientists have ever conducted, it has been proven that no such natural process exists. Never, in all the history of science, has even one tiny atom been created nor has even one tiny atom been annihilated.

Creation requires a supernatural process for bringing matter into existence. This implies that only a supernatural process can take matter out of existence. In the meantime, until the Creator is ready to take matter out of existence, it will all stay here. And that is precisely what the First Law of Thermodynamics, one of the two best proved laws of science, tells us. Men can change matter/energy around; we can turn coal into heat energy, and heat energy into electric energy, and electric energy into light energy, but we cannot create or destroy any of it.

Surely this is a humbling thought even to evolutionists. With all our modern technology, we still can't even destroy one tiny particle of matter, let alone create one. The barrier between existence and non-existence remains impenetrable. In fact we can't even imagine what is on the other side of that barrier. What is non-existence? Where is matter when it doesn't exist? Obviously, we are not dealing with natural processes, but with the supernatural.

Thus, while we cannot observe or re-enact either creation or evolution, and thus cannot establish either as a proven law of science, we can compare them to the First Law of Thermodynamics, which is a proven law. It is clear that creation is in perfect harmony with the First Law, and that evolution is in direct conflict with it. Since the First Law of Thermodynamics is one of the two best proved laws of science, this is powerful evidence in favor of creation.

THE SECOND LAW OF THERMODYNAMICS

Morris and Parker at page 201:

> Eddington also originated the term "Time's Arrow" to describe the Second Law, noting that the arrow points downward. If present processes continue to function into the indefinite future, eventually all energy will become useless, uniform, heat energy; all structures will have disintegrated into maximum disorder, their state of maximum probability; and all information will have become meaningless noise. The sun and stars will burn out, all processes will stop, and the universe will die an ultimate "heat death." It will still exist (by the First Law), but will be dead (by the Second Law).

Evolution claims to be a universal process of improvement, a universal organizing process, a natural process that has taken the universe from cosmic dust, or hydrogen gas, to its present complexity. Yet by every observation that scientists have ever made and by every experiment scientists have ever conducted, it has been proven that the universe is going in the opposite direction.

Creation claims that the supernatural Creator brought the universe into existence and organized it according to His own design. Energy was put where it would be used for accomplishing the Creator's purpose. And by every observation that scientists have ever made and by every experiment scientists have ever conducted, it has been proven that this is happening. Energy is being used and is becoming unavailable. The universe is not winding itself up, it is running down. Time's arrow points downward.

Again, we can compare the two faiths, creation and evolution, to a proven law of science to see which is a reasonable faith and which is unreasonable. Creation tells us that the universe moves from a highly organized state toward a state of disorganization. This agrees with the Second Law. Evolution claims the universe moves from a state of disorganization toward a highly organized state. This disagrees with the Second Law. The Second Law of Thermodynamics is more powerful evidence in favor of creation.

THE LAW OF BIOGENESIS

Louis Pasteur conducted experiments that proved that living organisms come only from other living organisms, and not from non-living matter. Countless observations and experiments have proven this to be true. Yet evolution requires spontaneous generation of life from non-living matter, that is, some natural process that can produce life from chemicals. If there is no spontaneous generation, then in order to get the first life into existence, supernatural creation is required. Again, evolution is in direct conflict with an

95

established law of science.

But evolutionists claim that billions of years ago, under different conditions, spontaneous generation of life did occur. They claim that over millions of years by chemical processes, there was a build-up of the basic organic compounds necessary for life; that these were gathered in ancient seas, forming a "pre-biotic soup"; and after more millions of years combinations were formed that were able to reproduce themselves, thus becoming the first living organisms. There is no evidence that this actually happened. It is simply something that evolutionists like to think might have happened. There are, however, three good lines of evidence that show it did not happen.

1. There is no trace of "prebiotic soup" in the sedimentary rocks. Quoting from Denton, pages 260-261:

> The existence of a prebiotic soup is crucial to the whole scheme. Without an abiotic accumulation of the building blocks of the cell no life could ever evolve. If the traditional story is true, therefore, there must have existed for many millions of years a rich mixture of organic compounds in the ancient oceans and some of this material would very likely have been trapped in the sedimentary rocks lain down in the seas of those remote times.
>
> Yet rocks of great antiquity have been examined over the past two decades and in none of them has any trace of abiotically produced organic compounds been found. . . . As on so many occasions, paleontology has again failed to substantiate evolutionary presumptions. Considering the way the prebiotic soup is referred to in so many discussions of the origin of life as an already established reality, it comes as something of a shock to realize that there is absolutely no positive evidence for its existence.

2. The "prebiotic soup" could not have formed if

there were oxygen in the atmosphere, nor could it have formed if there were no oxygen in the atmosphere. Denton, pages 261-262:

> In the presence of oxygen any organic compounds formed on the early earth would be rapidly oxidized and degraded. For this reason many authorities have advocated an oxygen-free atmosphere for hundred of millions of years following the formation of the Earth's crust. Only such an atmosphere would protect the vital but delicate organic compounds and allow them to accumulate to form the prebiotic soup. . . . But even if there was no oxygen, there are further difficulties. Without oxygen there would be no ozone layer in the upper atmosphere which today protects the Earth's surface from a lethal dose of ultraviolet radiation. . . . . What we have then is a sort of "Catch 22" situation. If we have oxygen we have no organic compounds, but if we don't have oxygen we have none either.

3. The amazing complexity of life precludes spontaneous generation. Denton, pages 328-329:

> To grasp the reality of life as it has been revealed by molecular biology, we must magnify a cell a thousand million times until it is twenty kilometres in diameter and resembles a giant airship large enough to cover a great city like London or New York. What we would see would be an object of unparalleled complexity and adaptive design. On the surface of the cell we would see millions of openings, like port holes of a vast space ship, opening and closing to allow a continual stream of materials to flow in and out. If we were to enter one of these openings we would find ourselves in a world of supreme technology and bewildering complexity. We would see endless highly organized corridors and conduits branching in every direction away from the perimeter of the cell, some leading to the central memory bank in the nucleus and others to

assembly plants and processing units. The nucleus itself would be a vast spherical chamber more than a kilometre in diameter, resembling a geodesic dome inside of which we would see, all neatly stacked together in ordered arrays, the miles of coiled chains of the DNA molecules. A huge range of products and raw materials would shuttle along all the manifold conduits in a highly ordered fashion to and from all the various assembly plants in the outer regions of the cell.

We would wonder at the level of control implicit in the movement of so many objects down so many seemingly endless conduits, all in perfect unison. . . . . What we would be witnessing would be an object resembling an immense automated factory, a factory larger than a city and carrying out almost as many unique functions as all the manufacturing activities of man on earth. However, it would be a factory which would have one capacity not equalled in any of our own most advanced machines, for it would be capable of replicating its entire structure within a matter of a few hours. To witness such an act at a magnification of one thousand million times would be an awe-inspiring spectacle.

Viewed through the microscopes available in Darwin's time, the cell appeared to a be rather disordered blob. But, as can be seen from Dr. Denton's description, we now know that the single cell is an object of incredible complexity. What is equally incredible is that modern scientists can still insist that life was accidentally produced by spontaneous generation.

Dr. Robert Gange, whose expertness is in physics and mathematics, in *Origins and Destiny*, Word Publishing, 1986, after describing the incredible complexity of a living cell and showing the mathematical impossibility of its formation by accidental means, stated the following at page 77:

> The groundless belief that life spontaneously arose from nonliving physical matter was rationally defended for centuries because no one had any information to the contrary. Now that is over, and we know better. Today, we can see inside living cells and study the resplendent majesty of a structure so awesome that it reeks of divine fingerprints. It's one thing to defend wrong beliefs out of ignorance, but it's quite another to perpetuate the folly when the light of day shows a more truthful way.

Sir Fred Hoyle's comment on this is worth repeating. Hoyle, page 23:

> In short there is not a shred of objective evidence to support the hypothesis that life began in an organic soup here on the Earth. Indeed, Francis Crick, who shared a Nobel prize for the discovery of the structure of DNA, is one biophysicist who finds this theory unconvincing. So why do biologists indulge in unsubstantiated fantasies in order to deny what is so patently obvious, that the 200,000 amino acid chains, and hence life, did not appear by chance?

The Law of Biogenesis tells us that life comes only from prior life. Creation agrees. The first life on Earth was created by a living God who enabled it to be fruitful and multiply and fill the Earth. Evolution, in direct conflict with the Law of Biogenesis, claims that life was formed accidentally. As Sir Fred Hoyle says, it is obvious that life did not appear by chance, and to think otherwise is to "indulge in unsubstantiated fantasies." Clearly the Law of Biogenesis is strong evidence in favor of creation.

Study Questions

1. Why is evolution important to the faith of secular humanism?

2. Explain why neither evolution nor creation can be established as a scientific law.

3. What should we know about experts upon whom we rely for scientific information?

4. Explain the First Law of Thermodynamics.

5. How does the First Law relate to evolution and to creation?

6. Explain the Second Law of Thermodynamics.

7. How does the Second Law relate to evolution and to creation?

8. What is the "prebiotic soup" theory and why have evolutionists developed this theory?

9. Why is the presence or absence of oxygen in the atmosphere a problem for the prebiotic soup theory?

10. Describe the complexity of a single cell and explain why this precludes spontaneous generation of life.

7

EVOLUTION, PART TWO

Are human beings created in the image of God, or are they accidental combinations of chemicals? Our answer to that question largely determines what we believe and how we live. If we evolved accidentally from chemicals, then secular humanism is a reasonable faith. But if evolution is false, then secular humanism is not only false, it is a dangerous and destructive pagan religion. Thus, evolution is humanism's most important doctrine, and for that reason it is vigorously taught and promoted as an established scientific fact.

Chapters six and seven set forth evidence to prove that not only is evolution not a scientific fact, it is not even a reasonable theory. Chapter six presented 3 lines of evidence, based on 3 established laws of science, to show that evolution is in hopeless conflict with all three of these laws, but that creation is in perfect harmony with all of them. In chapter seven we will consider 5 more lines of evidence, based on actual observation and scientific discovery, to show that evolution is unreasonable and false.

Darwin recognized many problems with his theory, but it was his expectation that future discoveries and scientific advances would prove him to be right. Just the opposite has happened. The more we discover and the more we learn, the more certain it becomes that the universe and all that is in it, including human beings, were created by a supernatural Creator.

THE STABILITY OF THE BASIC KINDS OF LIFE

Creationists believe that God created all of the different kinds of plant and animal life. In His wisdom, He provided mechanisms by which living plants and animals could change and adapt to changing environments, but could not go beyond their own kind. He gave each kind its own "gene pool" which is the chief means by which changes and adaptations are achieved.

By selective breeding it is possible to produce many different varieties within one kind of life. This has been done many times with both plants and animals. But is is not possible to produce a different kind. For example, by selective breeding, many different varieties of cattle have been produced. Desired traits have been developed by selecting for breeding stock, individuals possessing those traits. We have varieties that produce more meat, or more milk, or richer milk, or have no horns, or are resistance to disease, etc. But all of these different varieties are still within the cattle kind. No amount of selective breeding has ever produced a different kind.

Selective breeding produces different varieties within a kind by sorting through the gene pool which God gave to that kind. The process has been compared to sorting through a barrel of marbles of all different sizes to find the largest marble. Without looking you take out two marbles and discard the smaller. Then take out another marble and again discard the smaller. At first progress is fairly rapid, but as the retained marble gets larger, progress becomes slower, until at last the largest marble is found and change in size stops.

Of course the gene pool for any kind of life is vastly more complex that a barrel of marbles. But livestock breeders use selective breeding to sort through the gene pool in much the same way, at first making fairly rapid progress, and then slowing as the limits of the gene pool are approached. Beyond those limits they cannot go. Selective breeding cannot produce a different kind of life.

Evolution claims to be an ongoing, universal process producing new and more complex kinds of plants and animals. The means by which this is accomplished is natural selection. Within any kind of life are individuals that possess traits that give a survival advantage and thus these individuals live and produce more offspring to whom they pass these traits. So natural selection is selective breeding carried on by nature instead of man.

The classic example of natural selection, to which evolutionists always point, is the case of the peppered moth in England. In 1850, when the trees were covered with a mottled gray lichen, about 98% of the moths were gray colored. This color gave them excellent camouflage when resting on the gray lichen so they were less often eaten by birds, and thus lived to reproduce more light colored moths. But the environment changed. By 1950 air pollution had killed the lichen, and now the trees were darker so that now the dark moths had the better camouflage, and 98% of the moths were of the darker color.

Of course, the moths are still moths. A new kind has not been produced. Because of the change in environment, those moths possessing the genes for dark color became the principle breeding stock, just as livestock breeders may select cattle with genes for higher milk production to use for breeding stock. Thus natural selection can work under just the right circumstances. But, like artificial selection, natural selection works with the gene pool which God gave to the kind and cannot go beyond that kind. God, in His wisdom, provided this means for a kind to adapt and survive under changing conditions.

Evolutionists claim, however, that the gene pool can be changed by mutations. It is true that some kinds of radiation and certain chemicals can produce mutations by damage to the reproductive cells, and that these random changes can be passed on to future generations. Much work has been done with fruit flies, using x-ray to produce the damage and thus developing varieties of fruit flies with miniature wings, or vestigial wings, or with other deformities, but never producing anything but a fruit fly.

Science is based on observation. Certainly, very intense observation has been going on since 1859 (the year Darwin published his theory) as evolutionists have eagerly sought to prove that new kinds of life are produced by natural means. But the search has been to no avail. The basic kinds or types of life are completely stable. There can be many variations within the type or kind, but no new kinds of life have been observed.

Morris and Parker, page 119:

> If evolutionists really spoke and wrote only about observable variation within type, there would be no creation/evolution controversy. But as you know, textbooks, teachers, and television documentaries insist on extrapolating from simple variation within type to the wildest sorts of evolutionary changes. And, of course, as long as they insist on such extrapolation, creationists will point out the limits to such change and offer creation instead as the most logical inference from our observations. All we have ever observed is what evolutionists themselves call "subspeciation" (variation within type), never "transspeciation" (change from one type to others).

In *Darwin on Trial* at page 151, Professor Johnson, from his perspective as an expert in the fields of evidence and logic, commented as follows on this tactic of unlimited extrapolation which is used so often by evolutionists:

> Their most important device is the deceptive use of the vague term "evolution."
> "Evolution" in Darwinist usage implies a completely naturalistic metaphysical system, in which matter evolved to its present state of organized complexity without any participation by a Creator. But "evolution" also refers to much more modest concepts, such as microevolution and biological relationship. The tendency of dark moths to preponderate in a population

when the background trees are dark therefore demon-strates evolution — and also demonstrates, by semantic transformation, the naturalistic descent of human beings from bacteria.

If critics are sophisticated enough to see that popu-lation variations have nothing to do with major trans-formations, Darwinists can disavow the argument from microevolution and point to relationship as the "fact of evolution." Or they can turn to biogeography, and point out that species on offshore islands closely resemble those on the nearby mainland. Because "evo-lution" means so many different things, almost any example will do. The trick is always to prove one of the modest meanings of the term, and treat it as proof of the complete metaphysical system.

The stability of the different kinds of life is in per-fect harmony with creation. But it is in direct conflict with evolution. God is a Creator of order, not chaos.

FOSSILS

Evolutionists said the reason the different kinds of life appear to be so stable and we have never been able to see any new kind of life being formed, is that evolution happens too slowly to be observed. Evolu-tion requires millions and even billions of years. Therefore the only place to see evidence of the differ-ent kinds of life being formed is in the fossil record.

A fossil is any remains or traces of plant or animal life preserved in the rock formations of the earth's crust. The fossils, according to evolutionists, were deposited over the same billions of years that evolu-tion was taking place, and thus would give us the record of all the different kinds of life as they devel-oped from common ancestors. Paleontology (the study of fossils) would surely provide conclusive proof of evolution. Again evolutionists were to experience bitter disappointment.

Billions of fossils have been found, and if evolution did happen, certainly the evidence would be found here. In fact, for many years evolutionists claimed the fossil record did prove evolution, and fooled the public and even many scientists into thinking the evidence was there. Sir Fred Hoyle's comment on this is interesting. Hoyle, page 41:

> Undoubtedly one of the greatest scoops of the propagandists supporting Darwin immediately after publication of *The Origin* was to persuade not only the public, but even very competent scientists in fields other than biology and geology, that the fossil record supported the theory almost to the point of giving proof of its correctness. Yet the situation was quite otherwise, as Darwin himself recognized, since he devoted an entire chapter of *The Origin* to "the imperfection of the fossil record'."

It is true that fossils are generally found in groups of the same kind. Evolutionists say this is because the simpler forms lived earlier and left fossils and then died out and more complex forms came later and their fossils are found in higher layers. They have identified 12 major rock systems and have constructed a "geologic column" with the simple forms of life at the bottom.

Although this geologic column is widely reproduced in textbooks and museums, there are many problems with it. No where in the world is the complete column found. It is constructed in the minds of geologists from rock layers found in different parts of the world. In some places the so-called older layers are found on top of younger layers. Some layers contain "misplaced fossils" — that is, kinds of life found in rock layers that supposedly were laid down millions of years before that kind of life evolved. So called "polystratic fossils" are found — that is, fossils in a vertical position and extending through more than one rock layer — layers supposed to be millions of years apart.

Creationists say all this fossil arrangement is explained by the fact that different kinds of life live in different ecological zones, and thus their fossils are found in different groups even though they may all have lived at or near the same time. Furthermore, fossils are not formed by gradual deposition, but by sudden catastrophe such as a great flood or a volcanic eruption. This explains why fossils are sometimes misplaced and are sometimes found in a vertical position.

But the most striking characteristic of the fossil record is the absence of all the billions of intermediate forms that Darwin's theory calls for. If, as Darwin claimed, all living things gradually evolved from common ancestors, then billions of fossils should have been left of all those transitional forms — from invertebrates to vertebrates; from fish to reptiles; from reptiles to birds; etc. But they are not there. All of the billions of fossils that have been found are of distinct kinds.

Denton, page 162:

> Despite the tremendous increase in geological activity in every corner of the globe and despite the discovery of many strange and hitherto unknown forms, the infinitude of connecting links has still not been discovered and the fossil record is about as discontinuous as it was when Darwin was writing the Origin. The inter-

mediates have remained as elusive as ever and their absence remains, a century later, one of the most striking characteristics of the fossil record.

It is still, as it was in Darwin's day, overwhelmingly true that the first representatives of all the major classes of organisms known to biology are already highly characteristic of their class when they make their initial appearance in the fossil record.

Perhaps the most stunning blow a lawyer can receive is to have his star witness take the stand and testify for the other side. The fossil record has dealt just such a blow to evolution. If real visible evidence of evolution was to be found anywhere, it was to be in the fossil record. But it is not there. Instead the fossils reveal the sudden appearance of all the different kinds of life. The fossils testify in favor of creation.

NO SATISFACTORY MECHANISM FOR EVOLUTION

Under the right conditions it is possible for natural selection to occur. As with the peppered moths, natural selection can favor certain traits and cause that trait to predominate. But natural selection does not produce the different traits. It simply works to eliminate or suppress those traits that are less desirable. What produces the different traits upon which natural selection can operate?

One proposed mechanism for producing these different traits was Lamarckism. This was the theory that traits acquired by parents during their lifetime can be inherited by their children. Thus a wood cutter, who developed large arm muscles using the ax and saw, would have children with muscular arms. Repeated experiments proved that is not true. Changes in the body cells do not affect the reproductive cells.

Darwin then turned to the chance variations which are found in any kind of life, as the mechanism producing the different traits upon which natural selection can work. But, as seen earlier, these proved to be all part of the same gene pool and, while selective breeding could sort through this gene pool to produce new varieties within the kind, it could not go beyond the gene pool to produce new kinds of life. Even more telling against this theory, is the fact that such a process would produce gradual change that would have been amply recorded in the fossils. Of course, the fossil record shows just the opposite — no such gradual change occurred.

Next evolutionists turned to mutations — random damage to the reproductive cells — as the mechanism producing the different traits upon which natural selection can work. However, the reproductive cells are incredibly complex — far more complex than any machine built by man — and just as it is unlikely that a hammer blow to a computer would improve it, so it is highly unlikely that random damage to reproductive cells would improve the offspring. Of course, actual experience proved that to be true. The unfortunate offspring produced by mutant genes usually die at birth or shortly thereafter, and almost never are better able to survive. Thus they provided nothing upon which natural selection could work.

Conceding that large or macro-mutations would not work, evolutionists contended that small or micro-mutations could make very small changes in the offspring that might be beneficial and thus could be preserved by natural selection and become the mechanism for evolution. The first problem with this is that in order to produce a new kind of life, a long series of related mutations would be required. According to Morris and Parker, page 97, the odds against getting only 3 related mutations in a row are one in a billion trillion, and 3 related mutations wouldn't even make a good start toward producing a new kind of life.

And then there is still the fossil record. If new kinds of life were produced by a long series of micro-mutations, then the record of this would have to appear in the fossils — but it isn't there. Faced with this inconvenient truth, evolutionists have lately turned back to the unlikely mechanism of macro-mutations.

Morris and Parker, page 146:

> A new concept of evolution is outlined by Stephen Gould in *Natural History* for June-July, 1977, in an article titled "The Return of Hopeful Monsters." Gould, who teaches paleontology at Harvard, says, "The fossil record with its abrupt transitions offers no support for gradual change . . .". Then he goes on to propose that "Macroevolution proceeds by the rare success of these hopeful monsters, not by continuous small changes within populations."

This, the most recent of the evolutionary theories, is called "punctuated equilibrium." According to this theory, evolution proceeds by great leaps, with a whole new kind of life being suddenly produced by a macro-mutation, followed by long periods of equilibrium. But what an unlikely, absurd mechanism this is. Imagine the odds against hitting a computer a mighty blow with a sledge hammer and thereby turning it into a color television. Such odds would be insignificant compared to the odds against inflicting accidental damage to the reproductive cells of a reptile and thereby causing it to produce a bird. Then imagine the odds against such a thing happening twice within a short period, for if the hopeful monster is to reproduce there must be two of them, one who just happened to be a male and another that just happened to be a female hopeful monster.

Why do highly educated scientists even consider such far-fetched theories? Because, if secular humanism is to remain a viable religion, it must have evolution. The fossil record shows only distinct kinds of life. The transitional forms, the "missing links" envisioned by Darwin, are not there. The fossils support creation. God created the different kinds of life, male and female created He them. It takes a far-fetched theory to get around that truth. The complete failure of evolutionists to come up with a reasonable mechanism for evolution, is telling evidence against evolution.

INSTINCTS

Instincts are a real problem for evolution. Hundreds of strange behavior patterns exhibited by living creatures have defied explanation on evolutionary grounds.

Consider, for example, the Indian tailor bird that makes its nest from two leaves by punching holes in the edges and sewing them together with cotton fibers. Or the little water spider who lives in a diving bell made of silk. She breaths air and supplies her diving bell home by bringing down bubbles of air from the surface. How could natural selection teach such things as these? How many baby birds fell to the ground and how many baby spiders drowned while their parents were slowly learning the correct techniques? Or are we to suppose that some random damage to the reproductive cells suddenly endowed birds and spiders with such knowledge as this? The impossibility of explaining instincts by natural means, is one of the reasons that Sir Alister Hardy concluded that evolution must be guided by some spiritual force. He cited examples even more strange than those above.

Hardy, page 225:

> It concerns a little free-living freshwater flatworm called Microstomum which has only a very simple nervous system. It stores in the surface layer of its body the nematocysts or stinging-capsules which have been produced by cells in the body of the polyp Hydra upon which it feeds simply in order to obtain weapons to use for its own defense. When Microstomum has sufficient nematocysts it will no longer attack Hydra even if it is starving. When the hydra tissues have been digested, the nematocysts which so remarkably have not been discharged, are picked up by cells lining the stomach, the endoderm, and passed through to cells of the inner tissue, the so-called parenchyma; these cells, like wandering amoebae, now carry the nematocysts to the outer skin, the epidermis, where they are arranged and turned into position ready to fire the stinging threads like so many guns mounted ready to counter any attack.

How did this little flatworm learn that it could live a safer life by arming itself with stinging capsules from a hydra? How did it learn how to eat the hydra without setting off the stingers? How did the wandering cells inside the flatworm learn how to pick-up the stingers and transport them to the outer skin, arrange them where they were needed and aim them in the right direction? Clearly such behavior could not have developed gradually through natural selection. Until fully perfected, it would have had no survival value — in fact just the opposite.

Could this be the result of a macro-mutation? Could random damage to the genes that control development of the nervous system have resulted in a flatworm with all these skills? That is like asking if you could program into a computer the *Encyclopaedia Britannica* by hitting it with a hammer. But that is not the only problem evolutionists have. Sir Alister Hardy described elaborate instinctive behavior by sponges, which are animals that have no nervous system at all. (Hardy, page 226) How can a mutation change the nervous system of an animal that has no nervous system?

Countless examples of strange and wonderful instinctive behavior could be cited. How God has made animals, birds, fish, worms, spiders, sponges and single cells behave the way they do, we do not know. But we can see that God, in His wisdom, made these instincts so strange, so wonderful, so bizarre, that no reasonable person could believe they are the accidental result of evolution. Truly, as the inspired Apostle Paul wrote, atheists are "without excuse" (Rom. 1:20).

HOMOLOGY

Homology refers to parts of different kinds of life that are corresponding in type of structure, as the wing of a bat and the foreleg of a mouse are considered to be homologous. Evolutionists claim that all

these similar structures prove descent from a common
ancestor. Creationist argue that it simply shows design
by the same Designer. They say it is logical that creatures created to live in the same environment would
have similar organs, that is, similar lungs to breath the
same air, etc.
For many years evolutionists regarded homology as
one of their best arguments. Many charts were made
showing just how arms, front legs, wings, and flippers
all came from the same common ancestor. Evolutionists were sure that as we learned more about the
make-up of our bodies, the more homologous relationships we would find. But again they were doomed to
disappointment. Problems began to arise as biologists
learned more about genetics:
Hardy, pages 211 – 212:

When I was an undergraduate student just after the
First World War, and indeed when I was a professor in
the '30's, it all seemed so obvious. The same homologous structures must clearly be due to the same hereditary factors handed on generation after generation
from the early ancestor with occasional changes by
mutation; the wide variety of form seen in different
animal groups being due to natural selection acting
upon these factors or genes which were handed on,
with mutational changes, from the original ancestral
form. . . . In truth we can no longer say that homologous structures are always due to the same – homologous – genes, however modified by mutation, handed
on in the process of descent. Any animal structure we
are looking at is produced by the combined effects of
a particular gene-complex and the influence of the
environment in which the animal develops; and we
now find that what we have been calling homologous
structures are often produced by the action of quite
different genes.

115

In other words, the "scientific fact", taught in biology classrooms, that arms, front legs, wings, flippers, etc., are all due to the same hereditary factors handed down from a common ancestor, proved to be little more than wishful thinking when it turned out that such structures may be produced by quite different genes. But more serious problems for evolution were yet to come. With the development of the new science of molecular biology, evolutionists were confident that here at last they would find strong evidence of evolutionary relationships. Once again they were doomed to disappointment:

Denton, pages 277 – 278:

> On the other hand, the new molecular approach to biological relationships could have provided very strong, if not irrefutable, evidence supporting evolutionary claims. Armed with this new technique, all that was necessary to demonstrate an evolutionary relationship was to examine the proteins in the species concerned and show that the sequences could be arranged into an evolutionary series. . . . The prospect of finding sequences in nature by this technique was, therefore, of great potential interest. Where the fossils had failed and morphological considerations were at best only ambiguous, perhaps this new field of comparative biochemistry might at last provide objective evidence of sequence and of the connecting links which had been so long sought by evolutionary biologists.
>
> However, as more protein sequences began to accumulate during the 1960s, it became increasingly apparent that the molecules were not going to provide any evidence of sequential arrangements in nature, but were rather going to reaffirm the traditional view that the system of nature conforms fundamentally to a highly ordered hierarchic scheme from which all direct evidence for evolution is emphatically absent.

Dr. Denton, speaking from the perspective of his specialty, molecular biology, reached this conclusion: Denton, pages 290 – 291:

> There is little doubt that if this molecular evidence had been available one century ago it would have been seized upon with devastating effect by the opponents of evolution theory like Agassiz and Owen, and the idea of organic evolution might never have been accepted.
> This new era of comparative biology illustrates just how erroneous is the assumption that advances in biological knowledge are continually confirming the traditional evolutionary story. There is no avoiding the serious nature of the challenge to the whole evolutionary framework implicit in these findings.

Thus the whole study of homology and comparative anatomy, once thought to be strong evidence in favor of evolution, has now proven to be very strong evidence against evolution.

CONCLUSION

Other evidence against evolution could be presented, but the eight lines of evidence presented in chapters six and seven are probably the most important. These are all based on established scientific law and actual scientific observation and discovery. These eight lines of evidence are:

1. Evolution's direct conflict with the First Law of Thermodynamics.

2. Evolution's direct conflict with the Second Law of Thermodynamics.

3. The practical impossibility of spontaneous generation of life.

4. The stability of the basic kinds of life.

5. The absence of intermediate forms in the fossil record.

6. The lack of a satisfactory mechanism for evolution.

7. The inability of evolution to explain complicated instinctive behavior.

8. The absence of homologous relationships between different kinds of life.

Brief mention should be made of two arguments that were formerly used in support of evolution – the recapitulation theory and the vestigial organs theory. Both of these arguments were based on erroneous data, and are no longer used by knowledgeable evolutionists.

Morris and Parker, page 6:

> The old arguments for evolution based on the recapitulation theory (the idea that embryonic development in the womb recapitulates the evolution of the species) and vestigial organs ("useless" organs believed to have been useful in an earlier stage of evolution) have long been discredited.

In the final chapter of his book, Dr. Denton, compares the tenacity with which evolutionists defend their theory, with that of the medieval astronomers who believed that the Earth was the center of the universe. As the evidence piled up against them, these astronomers, instead of considering that their theory might be wrong, kept trying to explain the new evidence by modifying the theory until it became "a fantastically involved system entailing a vast and ever-growing complexity of epicycles."

So it is with modern evolutionists. As the evidence

mounts against them, they refuse to consider the alternative of creation, and instead devise ever more bizarre theories to explain away the obvious facts. The tragedy is that the general public is not informed of all the evidence against evolution. In fact, evolutionists have repeatedly gone to court to keep such evidence out of our public schools, and millions of people continue to believe that Darwin's theory is scientific fact.

Why do respectable scientists persist in this deception? Like the medieval astronomers, some are probably incapable of setting aside all they have been taught and accepting a wholly different way of thinking. But the basic cause is that set out at John 3:19; they refuse to come to the light because they love the darkness. They want to escape from God.

Study Questions

1. Since neither evolution or creation is a scientific law, how can we determine which is a reasonable faith and which is a blind faith?

2. What means did God provide to enable plants and animals to adapt to changing environments?

3. Explain why natural selection is not the same as evolution.

4. If evolution really happened, why should the fossil record provide the best evidence for it?

5. What is the most striking characteristic of the fossil record and why is this strong evidence against evolution?

6. Why are macro-mutations such a poor mechanism for evolution?

7. Why have evolutionists nevertheless been forced

to turn back to macro-mutations?

8. Why are instincts a difficult problem for evolution?

9. What effect has the new science of molecular biology had upon the evolutionary claim of homologous relationships between different kinds of life?

10. Why do millions of people still cling to the evolutionary faith?

8

THE BIBLE, PART ONE

Thus far our principle concern has been evidence for the existence of God, for the reality of the spiritual realm, and for the truth of supernatural events. We have seen within ourselves attributes — our self-consciousness, our ability to reason, our moral nature and our ability to choose — that set humans apart from all other forms of life on earth, and that cannot be explained if we are nothing but accidental combinations of chemicals. We have considered reports of miracles and spiritual experiences by many honest, sober-minded people, including carefully controlled experiments into various forms of extra-sensory perception, all of which defy explanation on materialistic grounds.

Most compelling of all, we have seen that the creation demands a supernatural creator. No natural process has ever been discovered or even conceived, that can bring anything into existence from non-existence. Nor has any natural process been discovered or even reasonably suggested, that can produce life from non-living matter. In fact we have considered eight extremely important lines of evidence based on established scientific law and actual scientific observation and discovery, and have seen that all of this evidence points to the truth of creation and the untruth of evolution.

The evidence we have considered up to this lesson is more than sufficient to convince a reasonable person that God does exist, that the spiritual world is real, and that supernatural events do occur. But this does not prove the truth of Christianity. It does not prove that the Bible is the Word of God or that Jesus is the Son of God. The remaining lessons are devoted to the evidence for these crucial issues.

THE PROBABILITY OF SUPERNATURAL EVENTS

Unbiased jurors are necessary for a fair trial. A juror's job is to listen to the evidence with an open mind and return a true verdict based on that evidence. A juror who has pre-judged any issue in the case, and thus does not have an open mind, is removed from the panel. Fairness demands the same open-minded approach to a study of the evidence for the truth and inspiration of the Bible.

Unfortunately, many people have rejected the Bible because they approach it with a bias against miracles.

Since the Bible does record many miraculous events, a juror who has already decided that miracles do not happen, will ignore the evidence and return a verdict against the Bible.

But this bias against miracles is not justified. To deny the possibility of miracles is to deny the existence of God. We have already considered the evidence that proves beyond a reasonable doubt that God does exist and that He brought the universe into existence by supernatural creation. Certainly the One who conceived and created the universe and all of its "natural" laws and processes, can intervene in His own creation and alter or set aside His own laws and processes.

If it is conceded that miracles are possible, this still does not prove that miracles actually happen. Most of us have never witnessed a *bona fide* miracle and we may not know anyone who has. The universe continues to operate in a uniform manner and it is easy to assume that it always has and always will. So men, especially those who wish to escape from God, find it easy to scoff at miracles, just as the Apostle Peter said they would:

> First of all, you must understand that in the last days scoffers will come, scoffing and following their own evil desires. They will say, "Where is this 'coming' he promised? Ever since our fathers died, everything goes on as it has since the beginning of creation." But they deliberately forget that long ago by God's word the heavens existed and the earth was formed out of water and by water (II Pet. 3:3-5).

Those who scoff at miracles do deliberately forget about the creation with all of its implications. The creation requires a supernatural Creator and, because the

123

effect cannot be greater than its cause, the Creator must possess everything that humans possess and much more. Since humans possess intelligence, our Creator also must possess intelligence, and since humans are able to communicate with others, our Creator also must have the ability to communicate.

Among all the forms of life placed upon the Earth, human beings are absolutely unique. We are a special creation, created in the image of God, and endowed with the unique ability to receive communications from our Creator. Having done all this, is it not reasonable to expect God to communicate with us? He gave us the ability to receive His message, surely He would send that message. He gave us the ability to choose between right and wrong, surely He would tell us how we should choose. He must have had some purpose for creating us, surely He would tell us how to fulfill that purpose.

But how can God communicate with us? How can we know that the word is really from Him? Moses asked that question 3500 years ago:

> Moses answered, "What if they do not believe me or listen to me and say, 'The LORD did not appear to you'?" Then the LORD said to him, "What is that in your hand?" "A staff," he replied. The LORD said, "Throw it on the ground." Moses threw it on the ground and it became a snake, and he ran from it. Then the LORD said to him, "Reach out your hand and take it by the tail." So Moses reached out and took hold of the snake and it turned back into a staff in his hand. "This," said the LORD, "is so that they may believe that the LORD, the God of their fathers—the God of Abraham, the God of Isaac and the God of Jacob—has appeared to you." Then the LORD said, "Put your hand inside your cloak." So Moses put his hand into his cloak, and when he

took it out, it was leprous, like snow. "Now put it back into your cloak," he said. So Moses put his hand back into his cloak, and when he took it out, it was restored, like the rest of his flesh. Then the LORD said, "If they do not believe you or pay attention to the first miraculous sign, they may believe the second. But if they do not believe these two signs or listen to you, take some water from the Nile and pour it on the dry ground. The water you take from the river will become blood on the ground" (Exod. 4:1-9).

Anyone claiming to have a message from God must first prove he is the authorized representative of God. His proof must be something that could not be duplicated by man. His proof must be something supernatural.

That there have been many false reports of miracles is not proof that real miracles do not occur. Anything genuine is always subject to being counterfeited. That most people have not seen a miracle does not prove that miracles never happen. If God caused miracles too often they would lose the power to authenticate His message. If they are to accomplish their purpose, miracles must be very unusual events.

To sum up:

1. The supernatural is possible because God exists.

2. The supernatural is probable because it is reasonable to expect a revelation from God, and it must be authenticated by something supernatural.

3. The fact that most people have not experienced a miracle is not a valid argument against miracles. We would expect miracles to be rare.

Thus, to reject the Bible on the ground that miracles do not happen, is not reasonable. If a miracle is testified to by good, competent, credible witnesses, there is no reason why that testimony should not be accepted. Lessons eleven and twelve will present in detail the evidence for the greatest miracle of all — the resurrection of Jesus Christ. Lesson ten deals with another kind of supernaturalism — fulfilled prophecy.

Lessons eight and nine present evidence which shows that the Bible is not an ordinary book, that it is not from the mind of man. Lesson eight deals with internal evidence, that is, evidence we can see from examination of the document itself, and lesson nine deals with external evidence, that is, evidence we can find from science, history, and archaeology. The purpose of all this is to prove beyond a reasonable doubt that the Bible is the Word of God, that Jesus is the Son of God, and thus that Christianity is true.

THE BIBLE CLAIMS TO BE FROM GOD

Over 3000 times the Bible claims its own inspiration. Typical of such claims are the following quotations, selected from 4 different Biblical writers and with some applying to the Old Testament and some to the New Testament.

All this took place to fulfill what the Lord had said through the prophet: "The virgin will be with child and will give birth to a son, and they will call him Immanuel"—which means, "God with us" (Matt. 1:22-23).

. . . and said, "Brothers, the Scripture had to be fulfilled which the Holy Spirit spoke long ago through the mouth of David concerning Judas, who served as guide for those who arrested Jesus . . . (Acts 1:16).

And we also thank God continually because, when

126

you received the word of God, which you heard from us, you accepted it not as the word of men, but as it actually is, the word of God, which is at work in you who believe (I Thess. 2:13).

Above all, you must understand that no prophecy of Scripture came about by the prophet's own interpretation. For prophecy never had its origin in the will of man, but men spoke from God as they were carried along by the Holy Spirit (II Pet. 1:20-21).

Bear in mind that our Lord's patience means salvation, just as our dear brother Paul also wrote you with the wisdom that God gave him. He writes the same way in all his letters, speaking in them of these matters. His letters contain some things that are hard to understand, which ignorant and unstable people distort, as they do the other Scriptures, to their own destruction (II Pet. 3:15-16).

Of course, we cannot prove the inspiration of the Bible just by what the Bible says about itself. But the fact that the Bible claims to be from God is very important for the following reasons:

1. If the Bible is the Word of God, we would expect it to so claim. We would think it strange if God gave us His revelation without telling us. If the Bible did not claim to be from God, that would certainly be evidence against its inspiration, evidence that men were trying to make it something that it is not.

2. Many of these claims were made when people were alive who had first hand knowledge of many of the events that were recorded and thus could have discredited the claims. Yet the claims were made and accepted.

3. The Bible teaches the highest moral and ethical standards, repeatedly condemning all falsehood and

deception. It is hard to believe that such a Book would make false claims about itself.

THE UNITY OF THE BIBLE

The Bible consists of 66 books written by some 40 different men of varied backgrounds and conditions. It was written by farmers, shepherds, fishermen, soldiers, prophets, scholars, politicians, and kings; it was written over a period of about 15 or 16 centuries; it was written in 3 different languages in several different countries; it was written in circumstances ranging from palaces to prisons. Yet the Bible has a unity of theme and teaching that makes it truly one Book.

Within the pages of the Bible a single main theme is being developed: the drama of redemption, the story of one great planned rescue operation. Despite the diversity of its separate units, the Bible tells this one story. There is a single plot being worked out; every section has its place in the unfolding of this plot. There is a beginning, a middle, and an end . . . .

The question that must be asked is this: in light of the Bible's great diversity, how can we explain this remarkable unity? What could have caused it? It is an accepted axiom of rational thinking that every effect must have sufficient cause. Not just any cause will do; the cause must be sufficient to produce the observed effect.

What is sufficient to explain the unity of the Bible? We must rule out chance; it is obvious that an intelligent purpose or plan is involved. Could a human mind be behind this plan? The great span of time rules this out. The unity requires a single mind behind the whole Bible, and no human being could have supervised a fifteen hundred-year project such as this.

Also it must be pointed out that this exciting drama

is not simply a piece of literature. It is not just on paper; it actually happened in history. The story unfolds not just on the pages of a book, but in actual lives and events in history. This gives an even deeper dimension to the unity of the Bible. It requires not just an author who could produce such a book, but also a director who could actually bring these things to pass in history, who could carry out a single plan involving several thousand years.

What is sufficient to explain it all? The only satisfactory answer is that both the plan and the book are of divine origin. Only the all-knowing, all-powerful God, who transcends history and to whom a thousand years is as but a day, could have written this drama on the pages of history and then caused such a varied collection of writings to tell it as one story.

The Authority of the Bible,
Jack Cottrell, Baker 1979

Consider this amazing example of the very thing Professor Cottrell wrote about. After the Jewish leaders had arrested Jesus and found Him guilty of the capital crime of blasphemy, they took Him to the Roman governor, Pilate, to get the Romans to carry out the execution. Then this exchange took place:

Pilate said, "Take him yourselves and judge him by your own law." "But we have no right to execute anyone," the Jews objected (John 18:31).

Pilate authorized the Jews to judge Jesus according to their own law which meant death by stoning. But the Jews did not want this. Earlier they had been prepared to stone the woman taken in adultery, and later they didn't hesitate to stone Stephen, but now they were suddenly very law abiding. Apparently it was part of their plan for Jesus to be executed the Roman way, that is, by crucifixion. To learn why, we must go back 15 centuries to the Spirit inspired writings of Moses.

> If a man guilty of a capital offense is put to death and his body is hung on a tree, you must not leave his body on the tree overnight. Be sure to bury him that same day, because anyone who is hung on a tree is under God's curse. You must not desecrate the land the LORD your God is giving you as an inheritance (Deut. 21:22-23).

Here is the key to the Jewish leaders' plan. They wanted Jesus dead, but they also wanted Him discredited so His followers would be dispersed and His teachings brought to nought. If He were stoned to death He might become a martyr. But, they reasoned, if He were crucified, that is, hung upon a tree, then He would be considered to be the lowest of criminals and under the curse of God, and thus completely discredited.

Earlier Jesus had provided another clue to this amazing puzzle when He made this prophecy to the Jewish crowd:

> "But I, when I am lifted up from the earth, will draw all men to myself." He said this to show the kind of death he was going to die (John 12:32-33).

Thus, Jesus told the Jews that He knew they were going to crucify Him, but made the astonishing prediction that instead of destroying His influence, as the Jews expected, His death on the cross would draw people to Him. Either not understanding Him, or not believing Him, the Jews went ahead and had Him crucified anyway.

The next piece of the puzzle is provided by Luke,

the inspired author of Acts, as he quoted the Apostle Peter before the Jewish Sanhedrin:

> Peter and the other apostles replied: "We must obey God rather than men! The God of our fathers raised Jesus from the dead — whom you had killed by hanging him on a tree. God exalted him to his own right hand as Prince and Savior that he might give repentance and forgiveness of sins to Israel. We are witnesses of these things, and so is the Holy Spirit, whom God has given to those who obey him" (Acts 5:29-32)

Here is the reason why the Jews' plan failed. God thwarted their scheme by raising Jesus from the dead and exalting Him on high. And what was the purpose of all this? For the final piece in this divine puzzle, we turn to the writings of Paul:

> Christ redeemed us from the curse of the law by becoming a curse for us, for it is written: "Cursed is everyone who is hung on a tree." He redeemed us in order that the blessing given to Abraham might come to the Gentiles through Christ Jesus, so that by faith we might receive the promise of the Spirit (Gal. 3:13-14).

Thus, from the writings of four different men, writing in different places and over a great span of time, we can piece together this whole wonderful story. Moses tells us that those capital offenders who are hung upon a tree are under God's curse, thus setting the stage, 15 centuries in advance, for Christ's atoning death on the cross. John quotes Jesus as making the amazing prophecy that His crucifixion, instead of driving people away from Him, would draw people to him, but despite this the Jews went ahead and insisted that He be crucified anyway. Luke quotes Peter as saying that although the Jews had Jesus hung upon a tree, God raised Him from the dead and exalted Him on high. And Paul tells us that Christ redeemed us by becoming a curse for us when He was hung upon the tree.

And just as Jesus predicted, the cross has been the great magnet, drawing untold millions to Him. As Professor Cottrell said, the story unfolds not just on the written page, but in actual lives and events in history. It is not possible that this could have come from a human mind. Only the all-knowing, all-powerful God could have directed such events, and caused different authors to write them down as one unified story. Truly this is the Word of God.

THE BIBLE'S FRANKNESS IN RECORDING THE WEAKNESS AND WRONGDOING OF ITS LEADING CHARACTERS

Enemies of the Bible have claimed that the Old Testament was written by Jewish partisans to exalt their nation and religion, and that the New Testament was written by Christians to glorify the Church.

But support for such claims is not found in the pages of the Bible. Instead we find in the Bible repeated accounts of the weakness and sinfulness of its leading characters — just the opposite of what we would expect if these were fictional accounts designed of advance the writer's cause. What Jewish writer, intent on producing a false history that would exalt his people, would record the two incidents when Abraham, the very father of the nation, denied that Sarah was his wife and turned her over to other men because of his own cowardice? Would such a writer have told us that Jacob, whose other name, Israel, became the name of the whole nation, was guilty of self-seeking duplicity when he tricked his brother out of his blessing; or that the patriarchs of most of the future tribes of Israel sold their younger brother into slavery; or that David, their greatest king, was guilty of murder and adultery?

No less striking is the honesty of the New Testament writers. They tell a very unflattering story about themselves, the very opposite of myth-mongers and legend-makers. All the twelve apostles doubted, were afraid, could not understand, forsook Christ in His extremity, and had to be rebuked by Him again and again; one of them betrayed Him; another, and he the chief one, denied Him with oaths. What a college of apostles, indeed, to represent Christ to the world and to carry His message to the ends of the earth!

Would a myth-maker or a fiction-writer have set forth such damaging facts? And would a conscious fabricator have done so? He might have known they would be used afterward against the imposture he was trying to foist upon the world.

This utter disingenuousness of the Biblical writers proves their integrity. Being honest, they told the simple, unvarnished truth; and if they told the truth, the divine inspiration and authority of the Bible are proved.

A System of Christian Evidence, Keyser,
The Lutheran Literary Board, 1953.

THE BIBLE'S BREVITY AND LACK OF COLORING

Consider these examples:

He told the crowd to sit down on the ground. Then he

took the seven loaves and the fish, and when he had given thanks, he broke them and gave them to the disciples, and they in turn to the people. They all ate and were satisfied. Afterward the disciples picked up seven basketfuls of broken pieces that were left over. The number of those who ate was four thousand, besides women and children. After Jesus had sent the crowd away, he got into the boat and went to the vicinity of Magadan (Matt. 15:35-39).

Picture a hungry crowd, far from any source of food, seated on the ground at His command, and then witnessing a miracle of creation of enough food for an "all you can eat" meal. Imagine the excitement of the crowd, and the vivid picture the author could have painted. Yet we are told simply that Jesus sent the crowd away and got into a boat and left.

Now picture a grief stricken mother and father, whose only daughter, a girl about 12, has just died. Jesus enters their home, commands the mourners to stop crying, and then this occurs:

But he took her by the hand and said, "My child, get up!" Her spirit returned, and at once she stood up. Then Jesus told them to give her something to eat. Her parents were astonished, but he ordered them not to tell anyone what had happened (Luke 8:54-56).

What a joyful scene this must have been. What a moving description could have been given of the tearful parents embracing their daughter, thanking Jesus, praising God; but Dr. Luke only says "her parents were astonished."

Flogging or scourging under Roman law was done with the flagrum, a multi-thonged whip weighted at the tips with bits of bone or metal which tore the flesh from the victims body. What a brutal, horrible scene it must have been when Jesus submitted to such savage treatment. Yet the Apostle John, under guidance of the Holy Spirit, reports it all in just 8 words:

> Then Pilate took Jesus and had him flogged (John 19:1).

When Paul and Barnabas came to Lystra, these pagan people thought they were gods and tried to worship them. But the fickle crowd soon turned against them with this terrible result:

> Then some Jews came from Antioch and Iconium and won the crowd over. They stoned Paul and dragged him outside the city, thinking he was dead. But after the disciples had gathered around him, he got up and went back into the city. The next day he and Barnabas left for Derbe (Acts 14:19-20).

A book could have been written describing the vindictiveness of the Jews, the brutality of the crowd, Paul's bruised and bleeding body, the tears and grief of the disciples, their overwhelming joy when Paul got up, and Paul's courage in going back into the city.

Why are these events treated in such a brief, matter-of-fact way? Certainly a human author would have built them up in order to further the cause. Did the Biblical writers lack eloquence and descriptive power? Were they cold, hardened men, devoid of normal human feeling?" One has only to read Paul's beautiful essay on love in 1 Cor. 13, or John's vivid descriptions of things to come in Revelation, to know this is not the case. Why then do we have these amazing omissions and lack of coloring? William Paley, in his fine old book, *Evidences of Christianity*, has the answer:

> Their whole soul was occupied with one object,

which predominated over the means subservient to it, however great those means might be. In the storm, the pilot's eye is fixed on the headland which must be weathered; in the crisis of victory or defeat, the general sees only the position to be carried, and the dead and the instruments of death fall around him unheeded. On the salvation of men, on this one point, the witnesses of Christ and the ministers of his Spirit, expended all their energy of feeling and expression. All that occurred — mischance, persecution, and miracle — were glanced at by the eye of faith, only in subserviency to this mark of the prize of their high calling . . . . Miracles were not to them objects of wonder, nor mischances a subject of sorrow and lamentation. They did all, they suffered all, to the glory of God.

Such singleminded concentration on the great theme of the Bible could only come from the guidance of the Holy Spirit. Truly this is strong evidence that the Bible is the Word of God.

THE BIBLE'S UNDESIGNED COINCIDENCES AND RECORD OF FAMILIAR DETAILS

To a layman it may seem that lawyers waste time in cross-examination by asking a lot of unimportant questions. But these "unimportant" questions can be very important in judging the truthfulness of a witness. False witnesses can rehearse their testimony so they will be in agreement on all of the important facts about which they know they will be questioned. But they cannot possibly think of all the small details that the opposing lawyer may include in his cross-examination. Thus, when two or more witnesses agree on these small, unexpected matters, it is obvious they are telling the truth.

Furthermore, the inclusion of a great deal of familiar detail is always the mark of an eyewitness account. Historians, as well as lawyers, recognize this and when, in the examination of ancient documents, they find undesigned coincidence and familiar detail, they treat that as strong proof of an authentic, eyewitness account.

Simon Greenleaf, the famous authority on the law of evidence and one of the chief builders of the fame of the Harvard Law School, in a book entitled *The Testimony of the Evangelists*, subjected the 4 Gospels to this kind of cross-examination. William Paley did the same for Paul's letters and the Book of Acts. Both men found that the Bible is replete with those familiar details and undesigned coincidences that are the infallible mark of true, eyewitness accounts. Some examples follow:

> You yourselves know that these hands of mine have supplied my own needs and the needs of my companions (Acts 20:34).

> To this very hour we go hungry and thirsty, we are in rags, we are brutally treated, we are homeless. We work hard with our own hands. When we are cursed, we bless; when we are persecuted, we endure it (I Cor. 4:11,12).

Here two different writers, writing at different times and at different places, both make passing reference to the fact that Paul worked with his hands. Are we to believe that Paul and Luke were clever and devious enough to deliberately plant this little detail in their respective accounts in order to fool readers of later centuries? How much more logical it is to believe that both simply told the truth.

Here is another example of one of those small, unexpected matters that are the hallmark of truthful accounts, this one involving 3 of the New Testament writers. The condition of an unfortunate woman with a chronic hemorrhage is described by Mark as follows:

> And a woman was there who had been subject to bleeding for twelve years. She had suffered a great deal under the care of many doctors and had spent all she had, yet instead of getting better she grew worse (Mark 5:25-26).

Luke's description of this same woman's condition is much less harsh on the doctors:

> And a woman was there who had been subject to bleeding for twelve years, but no one could heal her (Luke 8:43).

Obviously Luke had more sympathy for doctors than did Mark. The reason becomes quite clear when we read a casual remark made by Paul in his letter to the church at Colossae:

> Our dear friend Luke, the doctor, and Demas send greetings (Col. 4:14).

Here we see a perfect example of the type of familiar details and undesigned coincidences that lawyers and historians accept as strong proof of a truthful account. No reasonable person can believe that Mark, Luke, and Paul were clever enough to realize that future historians would look upon such details as evidence of the truth and so conspired to deceive future historians in this way. Even if they had been that clever and that devious, what possible motive could they have had for perpetrating such a fraud? How

138

much more reasonable it is to accept these passages for what they really are — evidence that all three men were telling the truth.

Consider Mark's account of what the angel told the women who went to the tomb on that first Easter morning:

"Don't be alarmed," he said. "You are looking for Jesus the Nazarene, who was crucified. He has risen! He is not here. See the place where they laid him. But go, tell his disciples and Peter, 'He is going ahead of you into Galilee. There you will see him, just as he told you'" (Mark 16:6-7).

Why did the angel say to tell his disciples "and Peter"? Was not Peter one of His disciples? The answer is found elsewhere. We know that Peter, after boldly assuring Jesus of his fidelity, had denied with oaths that he even knew Jesus, and had rushed off into the night weeping and broken hearted. No doubt Peter felt that he could no longer be included among the Lord's disciples. How typical of the compassionate Jesus that He would have His angel instruct the women to be sure and tell poor, broken hearted Peter that the victory was won and all was well. How perfectly and how beautifully those two words "and Peter" fit in with all that we know about Peter and about Jesus. Certainly this is the mark of a true account.

Consider yet another example. King Herod had James put to death and when he saw that this pleased the Jews, he had Peter arrested also. On the night before Peter's trial, as Peter lay in prison and as the church prayed for him, an angel appeared and removed the chains and led Peter out onto the street.

139

At first Peter thought he was seeing a vision, but when he realized he was really free, this occurred:

> When this had dawned on him, he went to the house of Mary the mother of John, also called Mark, where many people had gathered and were praying. Peter knocked at the outer entrance, and a servant girl named Rhoda came to answer the door. When she recognized Peter's voice, she was so overjoyed she ran back without opening it and exclaimed, "Peter is at the door!" (Acts 12:12-14).

It is easy to visualize this scene. Peter, then the Church's most prominent leader, is close to death and the Christians are in fervent prayer. Rhoda answers the knock and when she realizes it is Peter, she is so excited and overjoyed that she rushes back to tell the others, neglecting to open the door. A small detail, yet how true to life. Exactly the type of familiar detail that carries with it the mark of truth.

The Bible contains many such familiar details and undesigned coincidences as are always expected in truthful accounts. This is strong evidence that the Bible is true and thus, as it claims, is the Word of God.

JESUS, THE BIBLE'S CENTRAL CHARACTER

From Genesis through Revelation, the Bible presents the unfolding account of Jesus, the Messiah, the Saviour, the Son of God. If the Bible were written by the mind of man, then its authors, who repeatedly claimed to be writing by inspiration of God, were either badly deluded or blatantly dishonest. If so, then how could such men, or for that matter any human beings, have conceived of a character such as Jesus? Jesus was a humble carpenter in an obscure Galilean village. As far as we know, He had no formal education; He owned no property other than His tools and clothing; He never wrote any essays or books; He never held any kind of public office. He suddenly left His carpenter's trade and went about preaching for 3 short years, at the end of which He was executed as a criminal. From the human point of view, there was nothing about His life that points to greatness.

Yet it has been truly said that all the armies that ever marched, and all the parliaments that ever sat, and all the kings that ever reigned, put together, have not affected the life of man upon this earth as powerfully as has the one solitary life of Jesus. Only if all that the Bible says about Him, from His miraculous birth to His miraculous resurrection, is true, can this be understood.

Quoting again from Keyser's *A System of Christian Evidence*:

Among all the internal proofs of the divine inspiration of the Bible, the picture it gives of the person and work of Christ is the most important. The crucial question is, "Could mere human wisdom have conceived and depicted such a character?" Christ is both the puzzle and the stumbling-stone of the skeptics, just as He was of the ancient Jews and Greeks. How to account for Christ by merely natural and human means — that is the enigma.

Here are some pertinent questions: Why should anyone have wanted to invent Him and thrust Him upon the world as its Lord and Redeemer? How could deceivers have conceived a character of such purity and faultlessness? How could fanatics have fabricated one who was always sober, sane and poised in His traits, speech and demeanor? If He was what the Bible claims for Him, all is clear; every phenomenon is adequately explained. Otherwise He remains the insoluble mystery for science, philosophy and skepticism.

It is just inconceivable that Jesus could have been invented by men, and dishonest, deceitful men at that. It is much more reasonable to believe that He is the Son of God and that the Book that presents Him to us is the Word of God.

JESUS PUT HIS STAMP OF APPROVAL ON THE BIBLE

Jesus taught and preached here on Earth before the New Testament was written. But He made frequent use of the Old Testament and treated it as being Scripture and as being from the Holy Spirit. For example:

Jesus replied, "You are in error because you do not know the Scriptures or the power of God (Matt. 22:29).

He said to them, "How is it then that David, speaking by the Spirit, calls him 'Lord'? For he says, (Matt. 22:43).

He said to them, "This is what I told you while I was still with you: Everything must be fulfilled that is written about me in the Law of Moses, the Prophets and the Psalms" (Luke 24:44).

Jesus also affirmed the inspiration of the New Testament by promising the apostles that the Father would send the Holy Spirit to guide them into the truth.

But the Counselor, the Holy Spirit, whom the Father

will send in my name, will teach you all things and will remind you of everything I have said to you (John 14:26).

I have much more to say to you, more than you can now bear. But when he, the Spirit of truth, comes, he will guide you into all truth. He will not speak on his own; he will speak only what he hears, and he will tell you what is yet to come (John 16:12-13).

Proving the truth of Christianity can be done either by proving that the Bible is the Word of God or by proving that Jesus is the Son of God, because proof of one of these propositions necessarily proves the other. If the Bible is the Word of God, then Jesus is the Son of God because the Bible says so. Likewise, if Jesus is the Son of God, then the Bible is the Word of God because Jesus says so.

Thus it is very important that Jesus put His stamp of approval on both the Old Testament and the New Testament, because that means that all the evidence that Jesus is the Son of God, especially the great mass of evidence for His Resurrection, which will be presented in lessons 11 and 12, is also evidence that the Bible is the Word of God.

Study Questions

1. Why are miracles possible?
2. Why are miracles necessary?
3. Why is it important that the Bible claims to be from God?
4. Why is the unity of the Bible evidence that it is from God?

5. Why it the frankness of the Bible in reporting the wrong-doing of its leading characters evidence that it is from God?

6. Why is the lack of coloring in the Bible evidence that it is from God?

7. Explain what is meant by undesigned coincidences and why this is proof of the Bible's truthfulness.

8. Explain why it is unreasonable to believe that Jesus was invented by human beings.

9. Why is it important that Jesus put His stamp of approval on the Bible?

10. How did Jesus put His stamp of approval on the New Testament?

9

THE BIBLE, PART TWO

Is God the real author of the Bible? If the answer to this question is "yes", then Christianity is the true, and only true, religion from God, for, according to the Bible, God said, "You shall have no other gods before me" and Jesus said, "No one comes to the Father but by me." Thus, the evidence for the inspiration of the Bible is crucial to our whole study of Christian evidence.

In lesson eight, we looked at the internal evidence for the inspiration of the Bible. We considered seven remarkable facts or characteristics found within the Bible itself, which point to God as the real author. Other features of the Bible that point to its inspiration could have been named, but those given are probably the most important. Lesson nine is a study of the external evidence for the inspiration of the Bible, that is, evidence that depends, at least in part, on sources outside the Bible.

The Bible claims to be historical. It claims to relate actual events that occurred in the lives of actual people. Of course, the Bible does not present a review of ancient history. That is not its purpose. But the Bible does present the history of man's redemption by God, and in doing so,it does touch upon numerous events in human history. Thus, the Bible may be put to the same tests as other historical books. If it proves to be historically inaccurate then we cannot expect men to accept it as the Word of God. Certainly the Holy Spirit would not make mistakes in His record of historical events.

Furthermore, while the Bible is not concerned with the technicalities of science, it does contain incidental references to facts of nature which come within the realm of modern science. Here again, if the Bible is God's Word, it will not contain the scientific fallacies so common among ancient peoples.

Note, however, the affirmative side of this. If, in the 20th Century, men dig up clay tablets that have been buried for 3500 years and find writing thereon which confirms events or conditions recorded in the Bible; or if, in the 20th Century, men discover remarkable facts entirely unknown to scientists of just 100 years ago, only to find that such discoveries are in harmony with statements in the Bible written thousands of years ago; then we have powerful evidence that the Bible is indeed the Word of God. So these external evidences present not just a challenge, but instead more of an opportunity for defenders of the Bible.

THE BIBLE, PART TWO

THE SCIENTIFIC ACCURACY OF THE BIBLE

An excellent and very comprehensive study of the scientific reliability of the Bible is found in a book by Henry M. Morris, *The Biblical Basis for Modern Science*, Baker Book House, 1984. Dr. Morris, whose outstanding qualifications as a scientist are given in lesson six, made these statements in his introduction:

Men have too rapidly jumped to the conclusion that the Bible is unscientific (or "prescientific" as some would say). The Biblical cosmology has never been disproved; it has simply made men uncomfortable and been rejected. Nevertheless the actual facts of observation and experience can be shown to correlate with the Biblical view of the world and history in a highly satisfying way.

The Bible authors claim to have written the very Word of God, and it has been accepted as such by multitudes of intelligent people down through the centuries. This is more true today than ever in the past, and there are now thousands of qualified scientists around the world who quite definitely believe in the full verbal inerrancy of the Holy Scriptures. It is absurd for anyone to say that "science" has disproved the Bible.

Whenever a Biblical passage deals either with a broad scientific principle or with some particular item of scientific data, it will inevitably be found on careful study to be fully accurate in its scientific insights. Often it will be found even to have anticipated scientific discoveries.

Some examples of "anticipated scientific discoveries" follow:

Thus the heavens and the earth were completed in all their vast array. By the seventh day God had finished the work he had been doing; so on the seventh day he rested from all his work. And God blessed the seventh day and made it holy, because on it he rested from all the work of creating that he had done (Gen. 2:1-3).

Thus, we are told that creation is not a continuing process. It was a completed process — God finished. Modern scientists with all their modern equipment know that mass/energy is being neither created or destroyed. They call this the 1st Law of Thermodynamics. How did Moses, writing 3500 years ago, without telescopes or any scientific instruments for measurement, know this unless the Holy Spirit told him what to write?

Or how did the Psalmist, writing 3000 years ago know about the 2nd Law of Thermodynamics — that the universe is running down and wearing out:

In the beginning you laid the foundations of the earth, and the heavens are the work of your hands. They will perish, but you remain; they will all wear out like a garment. Like clothing you will change them and they will be discarded. But you remain the same, and your years will never end (Psa. 102:25-27).

Moses lived about 3500 years ago in a comparatively small area in Egypt and Arabia. Most of the animal species existing on the Earth were unknown to him. Yet he wrote that human beings are different from all others — a special creation, created in the image of God. Indeed, as we saw in lesson four, human beings are different in kind from all other forms of life, possessing spiritual qualities in common with God. How did Moses know this unless the Holy Spirit told him?

So God created man in his own image, in the image of

148

God he created him; male and female he created them (Gen. 1:27).

Without the benefit of modern chemistry how did Moses know that our physical bodies are composed of chemical elements that are found in the ground?

The LORD God formed the man from the dust of the ground and breathed into his nostrils the breath of life, and the man became a living being (Gen 2:7).

What is holding the Earth up? In view of the absurd answers given by other ancient peoples, how did the Biblical writer know the correct answer thousands of year ago?

He spreads out the northern skies over empty space; he suspends the earth over nothing (Job 26:7).

Modern medicine tells us that much illness is psychosomatic. In fact, many doctors believe that such things as worry, hate, envy, fear, and guilt cause or contribute to most illness. This is a new field in medicine, but consider what King Solomon wrote about it nearly 3000 years ago:

Trust in the LORD with all your heart and lean not on your own understanding; in all your ways acknowledge him, and he will make your paths straight. Do not be wise in your own eyes; fear the LORD and shun evil. This will bring health to your body and nourishment to your bones (Prov. 3:5-8).

Pleasant words are a honeycomb, sweet to the soul and healing to the bones (Prov. 16:24).

A cheerful heart is good medicine, but a crushed spirit dries up the bones (Prov. 17:22).

149

Today, anyone who watches the weather reports on television knows how wind currents move in circular fashion around high pressure and low pressure areas. We know how the water cycle works, with the moisture drawn up by evaporation and then condensed into rain, so the water runs in streams to the sea and then comes back again. But how could the Biblical writers, thousands of years ago, with virtually no means of long distance communication, with no knowledge of which way the wind was blowing even a few miles away, let alone in Greece or Persia, know about these vast wind currents and know about the wonders of the water cycle?

> The wind blows to the south and turns to the north; round and round it goes, ever returning on its course. All streams flow into the sea, yet the sea is never full. To the place the streams come from, there they return again (Eccl. 1:6-7).

> He draws up the drops of water, which distill as rain to the streams; the clouds pour down their moisture and abundant showers fall on mankind (Job 36:27-28).

Just in the last century, have physicists discovered that matter and energy are interchangeable. Now we are told that what appears to be good solid matter is really a sort of compressed energy, and is held together by powerful forces that keep the universe from blowing up. Of course when the New Testament was written nearly 2000 years ago, no human being knew these things. Then how could these writers have known that physical matter was made from something invisible and that it was necessary for it all to be held together?

By faith we understand that the universe was formed

150

at God's command, so that what is seen was not made out of what was visible (Heb. 11:3).

For by him all things were created: things in heaven and on earth, visible and invisible, whether thrones or powers or rulers or authorities; all things were created by him and for him. He is before all things, and in him all things hold together (Col. 1:16-17).

Other Bible passages could be cited that anticipate scientific discoveries of later centuries. Such things are not found in other ancient writings. Equally important is the fact that the Bible avoids the fallacies and scientific absurdities that are so common in other ancient writings. The odds against the Biblical writers getting all these things right by accident are astronomical. The only reasonable explanation is that these writers were guided to the truth by the Holy Spirit.

THE HISTORICAL ACCURACY OF THE BIBLE

1. As Tested by Ancient Historians

Judged even by human standards, the Bible writers are easily the most reliable of all ancient historians. The high ethical standards which they espoused, and their willingness to suffer persecution for what they wrote, attest to their truthfulness. Furthermore, the Biblical accounts are, by far, the most carefully preserved of all ancient documents.

But even apart from the Bible, such ancient writings as have been preserved, do confirm many of the important historical facts related in the Bible. Of even greater significance is this — we have no contemporary writings of any kind that refute any of the facts and events that are found in the Bible. Some examples follow:

The famous Roman historian, Tacitus (55 — 117 A.D.), who obviously despised Christians, wrote about the burning of Rome in 64 A.D. during the reign of Nero, and how Nero shifted the blame to the Christians and persecuted them for it. He wrote further,

> The name Christian comes to them from Christ, who was executed in the reign of Tiberius by the Procurator Pontius Pilate; and the pernicious superstition, suppressed for a while, broke out afresh and spread not only through Judea, the source of the malady, but even throughout Rome itself, where everything vile comes and is feted.

Note that Tacitus confirms the following important facts of Biblical history:
—There was such a person as Jesus.
—He was put to death by Pilate.
—He was executed as a criminal.
—The Christians derived their name from Him.
—Christianity arose in Judea and spread to Rome.
—Christians were a great multitude in Rome.
—Christians suffered terrible persecution in Rome.

Suetonius (69–140 A.D.), another Roman historian, wrote the Life of the Emperor Claudius, who reigned from 41 to 54 A.D. Suetonius wrote that Claudius "banished the Jews from Rome, who were continually making disturbance, Christus being their leader." Although Suetonius had some of his facts confused, not being quite clear on the distinction between Jews and Christians, he does confirm that Jesus was a very real and recent historical person, and that He was being preached among the Jews in Rome as being still alive and leading the new Church. We know from the Bible that it was this preaching that caused controversy among the Jews. As to the Jews banishment from Rome, Luke recorded this in Acts, as follows:

> After this, Paul left Athens and went to Corinth. There he met a Jew named Aquila, a native of Pontus, who had recently come from Italy with his wife Priscilla, because Claudius had ordered all the Jews to leave Rome. Paul went to see them (Acts 18:1-2).

Perhaps the most revealing account by an early Roman writer, is that written by Pliny the Younger (62 − 113 A.D.), who was governor of Pontus and Bithynia in Asia Minor on the southern shore of the Black Sea. He wrote a letter to the Emperor Trajan, who reigned from 98 to 117 A.D., seeking advice about what to do with the large number of Christians whom he had been persecuting. From some who had recanted under torture, he had learned the following:

> They affirmed that the whole of their fault, or error, lay in this, that they were wont to meet together on a stated day before it was light and sing among themselves, alternately, a hymn to Christ, as God, and bind themselves by an oath, not to the commission of any wickedness, but not to be guilty of theft, or robbery, or adultery, never to falsify their word, nor to deny a pledge committed to them when called upon to return it. When these things were performed it was their custom to separate, and then to come together again to a meal, which they ate in common without any disorder.

Perhaps Pliny realized that the Romans were torturing and killing their best, most law-abiding subjects, as he wrote further:

Suspending, therefore, all judicial proceedings, I have recourse to you for advice; for it has appeared to me a matter highly deserving consideration, especially on account of the great number of persons who are in danger of suffering; for many of all ages and every rank, of both sexes likewise, are accused. Nor has the contagion of this superstition seized cities only, but the lesser towns also, and the open country.

Truly the early Christians were people sanctified, that is, set apart to God, shining lights in a pagan world. Note that Pliny confirms the following facts about the early Church, all of which are taught in the Bible:

—That the Christians met together on a certain day.
—That they sang hymns together.
—That they worshipped Christ as God.
—That they practiced honesty and high morals.
—That they shared a common meal or communion.
—That they ate without the drunken disorder typical of the pagan feasts.
—That great numbers had been won to Christ.
—That many were prepared to suffer and die for Christ.
—That the Gospel of Christ had an universal appeal to all ages, all ranks, both sexes, and in both urban and rural areas. (There is neither Jew nor Greek, slave nor free, male nor female, for you are all one in Christ Jesus, Gal. 3:28).

A man named Thallas, who was born in Samaria, wrote at Rome about 52 A.D. No copies of his writings have been preserved, but reference is made to them by Julius Africanus, a second century writer, who, in discussing the darkness that occurred when Jesus was being crucified, said, "Thallas, in Book Three of his history, explains away the darkness as an eclipse of the sun — unreasonably as it seems to me." This shows that the events surrounding the crucifixion of Jesus were well know even at Rome some 20 years after they occurred.

The famous Jewish historian, Josephus (37 — 100 A.D.), as would be expected, had a better understanding of events occurring in Bible lands during the first century than did the Roman writers. He wrote about many of the same people who are found in the Bible and confirmed several of the events described in the New Testament. Although Josephus was not a Christian, he had this to say about Jesus:

> At that time lived Jesus, a wise man, if he may be called a man, for he performed many wonderful works. He was a teacher of such men as received the truth with pleasure. He drew over to him many Jews and Gentiles. This was the Christ; and when Pilate, at the instigation of the chief men among us, had condemned him to the cross, they who before had conceived an affection for him did not cease to adhere to him; for on the third day he appeared to them alive again, the divine prophets having foretold these and many wonderful things concerning him. And the sect of the Christians, so called from him, subsists to this time.

In this short passage, Josephus confirms the following facts about Jesus:
—That He was a wise man.
—That He performed many miracles.
—That He was a teacher of truth.
—That many followed Him.
—That He was the Christ.

—That Pilate condemned Him to the cross.
—That this was done at the instigation of the Jewish leaders.
—That on the third day He arose from the tomb.
—That His followers adhered to Him after the Resurrection.
—That the Christians were named for Him and so continued.

Other contemporary historians could be cited. Particularly reliable are early Christian historians such as Clement of Rome, Polycarp, Ignatius, and Justin Martyr, the last three of whom were willing to die for the truth of what they wrote. They confirm many of the facts related in the Bible. However, since they all wrote about the Resurrection of Christ, quotations from their writings will be saved for that study.

Although comparatively few historical writings from Bible times have been preserved to our time, those that we have do confirm the historical accuracy of the Bible. And as noted before, there is no contemporary history that refutes anything found in the Bible.

2. As Tested by Archaeology

Archaeology is the scientific study of the life and culture of ancient peoples, as by excavation of ancient sites, relics, artifacts, etc. It is a young science, most of its accomplishments having been made in the last two centuries.

Of course, archaeologists have not found specific confirmation for everything in the Bible. That would be too much to expect. But they have found specific confirmation for a considerable number of Bible statements, and have found general confirmation for many conditions and customs mentioned in the Bible.

Considering the natural destructive power of the elements over thousands of years, and the deliberate destruction by rulers who wanted to wipe-out all memory of prior regimes, and by grave robbers and vandals, it is only in the providence of God that so much has been preserved. The following is quoted from *Archaeology and the Old Testament*, Zondervan, 1954, by Merrill F. Unger, Th.D., Ph.D., a leading authority in the field of Biblical Archaeology.

Before the advance of research in Biblical lands, especially in the last half century, reams of what has been subsequently proved by archaeology to be sheer nonsense were written by scholars who viewed the Bible as legend, myth, or at best unreliable history. Acting as a corrective and a purge, archaeology has exploded many of these erratic theories and false assumptions that used to be paraded in scholarly circles as settled facts. No longer can higher critics, for example, dismiss the Hebrew patriarchs as mere legendary figures or deny that Moses could write. Archaeology has shown the falsity of both these and numerous other extreme contentions. Illuminating evidence is now available that Abraham, Isaac and Jacob were historical persons, as Genesis describes them. As for Moses, not only could he have written documents in Egyptian hieroglyphics, as his early residence in Egypt would indicate, or in Akkadian, as the Amarna Letters of the fourteenth century B. C. show, but in ancient Hebrew as well, as the discovery of the Ugaritic literature at Ras Shamra in North Syria (1929-1937) demonstrates.

Regarding authentication of the Bible, such confirmation may be general or specific. Examples of general confirmation are innumerable. For instance, excavations at Shiloh, Gibeah, Megiddo, Samaria and other Palestinian sites have fully corroborated the

Biblical notices of these cities. Cases of specific confirmation, while, of course, not as numerous as those of general corroboration, are nevertheless more striking.

Specific confirmation by archaeology can be spectacular. For example, the Bible tells how Nebuchadnezzar, king of Babylon, conquered the Jews and put Jehoiachin, king of Judah, in prison at Babylon. However, Nebuchadnezzar's successor took Jehoiachin out of prison and gave him a regular ration for life.

In the thirty-seventh year of the exile of Jehoiachin king of Judah, in the year Evil-Merodach became king of Babylon, he released Jehoiachin from prison on the twenty-seventh day of the twelfth month. He spoke kindly to him and gave him a seat of honor higher than those of the other kings who were with him in Babylon. So Jehoiachin put aside his prison clothes and for the rest of his life ate regularly at the king's table. Day by day the king gave Jehoiachin a regular allowance as long as he lived (II Kings 25:27-30).

About 2500 years later, archaeologists unearthed a clay tablet at the ruins of Babylon, that gave a list of those to whom rations were paid. Among the names was "Yaukin, king of the land of Yahud" which, translated to Hebrew is "Jehoiachin, king of the land of Judah." Surely God had a hand in preserving that fragile bit of evidence for 25 centuries.

Prior to 1843, the only reference found anywhere to an Assyrian king named "Sargon" was the following:

In the year that the supreme commander, sent by Sargon king of Assyria, came to Ashdod and attacked and captured it (Isa. 20:1).

Since no non-Biblical source mentioned Sargon,

hostile critics cited this passage as proof that the Bible was not history, but myth. Then, in 1843, Paul Emile Botta discovered Sargon's palace, and today Sargon is one of the best known of the Assyrian kings.

Until near the end of the nineteenth century, the Hittites were unknown in secular history. Yet the Bible mentions them 48 times and presents them as a numerous and powerful race. Hostile critics argued that it was impossible for such a people to disappear without leaving a trace, and cited this as proof of the Bible's unreliability. But again, archaeology proved to be the critics' undoing, as numerous finds culminated in the discovery of the capital of the great Hittite nation in modern Turkey.

Another alleged error in the Bible involved Belshazzar, king of Babylon:

> For a long time the fact that the Book of Daniel makes Belshazzar king at the time of the fall of Babylon (Dan. 5) instead of Nabonidus, as the cuneiform records show, was held as strong evidence against the historicity of the sacred account. The solution of this so-called discrepancy was apparent when evidence was uncovered not only indicating Belshazzar's association with Nabonidus on the throne but also demonstrating that during the last part of his reign the latter resided in Arabia and left the conduct of the kingdom of Babylon to his eldest son Belshazzar. (Unger, *supra*)

Other examples of specific confirmation of the Bible by archeological discoveries could be given. A much greater volume of general confirmations could be cited. While they are not as spectacular, the general confirmations are extremely important, because they show that the Bible presents a true and correct picture of the peoples, laws, customs, conditions, etc., which prevailed at the various periods involved. It would have been impossible for a forger, writing many centuries later, to have done this.

The science of archaeology has done much to confirm and illuminate the Bible, and much to silence its critics. Also important is the fact, that of all the thousands of archeological discoveries, none has refuted any part of the Bible. Archaeology provides strong evidence that the Bible is true, and therefore is the Word of God.

3. As tested by Historical Standards

This point involves evidence for the historical accuracy of the Bible by applying to it the methods and standards used by historians to test the credibility of ancient writings. Whereas the evidence from archaeology is more applicable to the Old Testament, this evidence applies especially to the New Testament.

a. Are they contemporary accounts — that is, were they written and published at or near the time of the events they record? This is important because the initial readers would know whether the accounts were true or not, and thus their acceptance of the accounts is strong evidence of truth. It is generally accepted that all of the New Testament was written in the 1st century A.D., and that it was accepted by many people who were familiar with the events it records.

b. Were they written and published at the place where the events happened? Again this is important because the initial readers would know if the accounts were true or not. It is clear that the New Testament was widely circulated in Palestine and the rest of the Roman world where the events occurred.

c. Were they written by persons in a position to

know the truth? It is clear that the New Testament was written by eye witnesses or by persons in close contact with eye witnesses.

d. Do the writings purport to recount public, widely known events? This is important because, if so, then not just a select group, but the general public would know whether the accounts were true or false. Much of Jesus' ministry and many of the other New Testament events occurred in public before large crowds. They occurred at the very crossroads of 3 continents, and most occurred in the largest and most important cities of the area. They could hardly have been more public.

e. Do the writings give specific details, such as names, dates, places, circumstances, etc.? False writings tend to be vague, so that it will be difficult to check them out. But the Bible gives the names of the people involved, the places where events occurred, the names of rulers, and other details that tie it securely to history. It can be checked out.

f. Do the writings call for action and did such action occur among the initial readers? If the initial readers, who were in a position to know the truth, all ignore the call for action, this tends to discredit the writings. But if large numbers respond to the call for action, especially if this response calls for drastic changes in their lives, then this is strong evidence of the truth of the writings. Of course, this is exactly what happened in the early Church. Thousands of people who had seen and heard Jesus, and who had witnessed many of the New Testament events, responded to the call for action even though it meant loss of jobs, confiscation of property, exile, persecution, and even martyrdom. What other historical records were tested by the torture and death of the historians and of many of those who witnessed their history?

g. Do the writings fit into the over-all fabric of history? Every important event that actually occurs is connected to other events that precede and follow it. There is a cause and effect relationship that cannot be faked. To falsely insert the story of Jesus into the history of the world is impossible. His life was lived at the crossroads of the ancient world, where the Hebrew, Greek, and Roman cultures all met, and His life had a vast and immediate effect on all 3 cultures. Take out the life of Jesus, and much of history becomes unexplainable.

All these standards for testing credibility point to the truth and accuracy of the Bible. Add to this the testimony of contemporary historians, and the testimony of archaeology, and we have powerful proof of the historical accuracy of the Bible. And if the Bible is true and accurate, then it is the inspired Word of God, because, (1) it records supernatural events that could come only from God, and, (2) it repeatedly claims to be from God.

Study Questions

1. Why is the historical and scientific accuracy of the Bible important to us?

2. Compare Bible references to scientific matters with those found in other ancient writings.

3. Name some scientific principles that were anticipated in the Bible.

4. Using evidence only from pagan writers, refute the claim that no such person as Jesus ever lived.

5. Name some important facts about the early Church that are revealed in Pliny's letter to Trajan.
6. What is meant by general confirmation of the Bible by archaeology? Give some examples.
7. What is meant by specific confirmation of the Bible by archaeology? Give some examples.
8. Why is it important that the New Testament was written at or near the time and place of the events it records?
9. Why is it important that the New Testament gives many details of the events it records?
10. How do the events recorded in the New Testament fit into the overall fabric of history and why is this important?

10

FULFILLED PROPHECY

The many lines of internal evidence presented in lesson eight and the external evidence presented in lesson nine, are enough to convince most people that the Bible is the Word of God. But the two most conclusive proofs remain to be covered. They are fulfilled prophecy, and, the resurrection of Jesus.

There are two ways God can attest His revelation to man — by miracles, and, by fulfilled prophecy. Miracles are of greatest value to those who actually witness them. Prophecy is of greatest value to those who can see its fulfillment. Today, we have the testimony of those who witnessed the Biblical miracles, and, while we were not privileged to see those miracles, we can test that testimony by the accepted rules of evidence.

In addition, we have the advantage of seeing how hundreds of Bible prophecies have been fulfilled.

Peter wrote to early Christians, who had seen the fulfillment of many prophecies, that they had the word of the prophets "made more certain", and thus it was to them evidence of the truth like "a light shining in a dark place."

> And we have the word of the prophets made more certain, and you will do well to pay attention to it, as to a light shining in a dark place, until the day dawns and the morning star rises in your hearts. Above all, you must understand that no prophecy of Scripture came about by the prophet's own interpretation. For prophecy never had its origin in the will of man, but men spoke from God as they were carried along by the Holy Spirit (II Pet. 1:19-21).

Prophecy is powerful proof because, as Peter emphasized, it must come from God. Only God knows the future. For example, consider the dismal record of economic forecasters and political pundits in our own time. Who can tell us what the stock market will be doing a year from now, or even a month away? Or who can name our president 20 years from now, or tell us what world events will occur even in the next year?

Yet the Bible contains hundreds of prophecies, some fulfilled in a few years, some not for centuries. And God made it clear that this is a sure mark of His truth, and challenged the false gods of paganism:

> "Present your case," says the LORD. "Set forth your arguments," says Jacob's King. "Bring in your idols to tell us what is going to happen. Tell us what the former things were, so that we may consider them and know their final outcome. Or declare to us the things

to come, tell us what the future holds, so we may know that you are gods. Do something, whether good or bad, so that we will be dismayed and filled with fear. But you are less than nothing and your works are utterly worthless; he who chooses you is detestable (Isa. 41:21-24).

PROPHECIES CONCERNING CHRIST

The most important and most abundant prophecies in the Bible are those concerning Christ. The Old Testament contains over 300 of these Messianic prophecies. In their preaching and writing, the apostles made frequent reference to the Old Testament passages concerning the coming Messiah, and how they had been fulfilled in the life of Jesus.

Jesus also stressed the importance of the Old Testament prophecies concerning the coming Messiah, and even chided His followers for being surprised when these prophecies were fulfilled in His life.

He said to them, "How foolish you are, and how slow of heart to believe all that the prophets have spoken! Did not the Christ have to suffer these things and then enter his glory?" And beginning with Moses and all the Prophets, he explained to them what was said in all the Scriptures concerning himself (Luke 24:25-27).

Some examples of Messianic prophecies follow:

The LORD had said to Abram, "Leave your country, your people and your father's household and go to the land I will show you. I will make you into a great nation and I will bless you; I will make your name great, and you will be a blessing. I will bless those who bless you, and whoever curses you I will curse;

167

and all peoples on earth will be blessed through you"
(Gen. 12:1-3).

And you are heirs of the prophets and of the covenant
God made with your fathers. He said to Abraham,
'Through your offspring all peoples on earth will be
blessed' (Acts 3:25).

When Moses wrote this Genesis passage, the Jews
were God's chosen people, and any prediction that all
peoples would be blessed through them was foreign
to their thinking. Even when Peter repeated this
prophecy 15 centuries later (as recorded in the verse
from Acts) he had no idea that the Gospel message
was for non-Jews too. Yet, within a few years the fulfillment began and continues to our own time – peoples all over the earth are being blessed by the Good
News about a descendent of Abraham.

"See, I will send my messenger, who will prepare the
way before me. Then suddenly the Lord you are seeking will come to his temple; the messenger of the
covenant, whom you desire, will come," says the LORD
Almighty (Mal. 3:1).

Here, centuries before Christ, the prophet stated that
a messenger would be sent to prepare His way, obviously fulfilled by John the Baptist, and states that the
Lord would come suddenly into His temple, which He
did. Since the temple was destroyed by the Romans in
70 A.D., this was also a prediction that the Messiah
would come before that date.

But you, Bethlehem Ephrathah, though you are small
among the clans of Judah, out of you will come for me
one who will be ruler over Israel, whose origins are
from of old, from ancient times (Micah 5:2).

168

Again, centuries before Christ, the prophet names the little village where He would be born.

For to us a child is born, to us a son is given, and the government will be on his shoulders. And he will be called Wonderful Counselor, Mighty God, Everlasting Father, Prince of Peace. Of the increase of his government and peace there will be no end. He will reign on David's throne and over his kingdom, establishing and upholding it with justice and righteousness from that time on and forever. The zeal of the LORD Almighty will accomplish this (Isa. 9:6-7).

Isaiah, writing about 7 centuries before Christ, tells us that He would be a Mighty God, etc., and that He would be an eternal King, the increase of His government never ending. Yet the same prophet wrote these words about the coming Messiah:

He was despised and rejected by men, a man of sorrows, and familiar with suffering. Like one from whom men hide their faces he was despised, and we esteemed him not. Surely he took up our infirmities and carried our sorrows, yet we considered him stricken by God, smitten by him, and afflicted. But he was pierced for our transgressions, he was crushed for our iniquities; the punishment that brought us peace was upon him, and by his wounds we are healed. We all, like sheep, have gone astray, each of us has turned to his own way; and the LORD has laid on him the iniquity of us all. He was oppressed and afflicted, yet he did not open his mouth; he was led like a lamb to the slaughter, and as a sheep before her shearers is silent, so he did not open his mouth. By oppression and judgment he was taken away. And who can speak of his descendants? For he was cut off from the land of the living; for the transgression of my people he was stricken. He was assigned a grave with the wicked, and with the rich in his death, though he had done no violence, nor was any deceit in his mouth. Yet it was the LORD'S will to crush him and cause him to suffer, and though the LORD makes his life a guilt offering, he will see his offspring and prolong his days, and the will of the LORD will prosper in his hand. After the suffering of his soul, he will see the light of life and be satisfied; by his knowledge my righteous servant will justify many, and he will bear their iniquities. Therefore I will give him a portion among the great, and he will divide the spoils with the strong, because he poured out his life unto death, and was numbered with the transgressors. For he bore the sin of many, and made intercession for the transgressors (Isa. 53:3-12).

How could the same Messiah be a Mighty God and an Eternal King, yet also be despised and rejected by men and be cruelly put to death? The Jewish scribes wrestled with this paradox for centuries without finding the answer, but now that it has all been fulfilled, we can see how beautifully it all came to pass in the life of Jesus.

When prophecy contains numerous detail, all of which is exactly fulfilled, that is infallible proof that the prophecy is from God. Consider some of the detail contained in this passage from Isaiah, all of which we know, from many sources, was exactly fulfilled:

—He was despised and rejected.

—He was a man of sorrows.

—He was pierced, beaten and wounded.

—He did not defend Himself from the Jews' accusations.

—He died under judicial sentence and not by mob violence or at the hand of an assassin.

—He died with criminals.

—He was buried by a rich man.

—After the suffering He would see the light of life.
—He would be satisfied with the result of His suffering.
—His suffering would save many.
—He would be exalted because of His suffering. Consider this detailed description of the crucifixion, written by David a thousand years before Christ, long before the Romans had devised this cruel method of execution. David couldn't have known this on his own and probably did not understand what he wrote. Yet he vividly describes the agony of the cross, the piercing of the hands and feet, the bones out of joint, the pressure in the chest, the dehydration. He describes the enemies of Jesus surrounding the cross to mock Him and even quotes some of the insults they would hurl. He actually foretold that the soldiers would divide His garments among them, casting lots for the best piece of clothing.

But I am a worm and not a man, scorned by men and despised by the people. All who see me mock me; they hurl insults, shaking their heads: "He trusts in the LORD; let the LORD rescue him. Let him deliver him, since he delights in him." Yet you brought me out of the womb; you made me trust in you even at my mother's breast. From birth I was cast upon you; from my mother's womb you have been my God. Do not be far from me, for trouble is near and there is no one to help. Many bulls surround me; strong bulls of Bashan encircle me. Roaring lions tearing their prey open their mouths wide against me. I am poured out like water, and all my bones are out of joint. My heart has turned to wax; it has melted away within me. My strength is dried up like a potsherd, and my tongue sticks to the roof of my mouth; you lay me in the dust of death. Dogs have surrounded me; a band of evil men has encircled me, they have pierced my hands and my feet. I can count all my bones; people stare and gloat over me. They divide my garments among them and cast lots for my clothing (Psa. 22:6-18).

For an amazing example of the minute detail contained in some prophecy, note the last sentence of this passage from Psalm 22. "They divide my garments among them and cast lots for my clothing." Here the Holy Spirit seems to contradict himself. First He says they will divide Christ's garments among themselves, and then He says they will cast lots for the clothing. Which will it be? For the answer we turn to John's Gospel:

When the soldiers crucified Jesus, they took his clothes, dividing them into four shares, one for each of them, with the undergarment remaining. This garment was seamless, woven in one piece from top to bottom. "Let's not tear it," they said to one another. "Let's decide by lot who will get it." This happened that the scripture might be fulfilled which said, "They divided my garments among them and cast lots for my clothing." So this is what the soldiers did (John 19:23-24).

Remember, David wrote this amazing bit of prophetic detail about 1000 years before it happened exactly as he had written. Can there be any reasonable doubt that the Holy Spirit told David what to write?

The claim has been made that Jesus deliberately set about fulfilling the Old Testament prophecies. Note that this is an admission that Jesus did fulfill them, and it is also an admission that this country carpenter was at least a genius, who had better understanding of the scriptures than all the Jewish wise men. But, of course, the answer to this charge is the obvious fact that many of these prophecies were fulfilled by His enemies, persons over whom He had no control. Paul pointed this out in the synagogue in Pisidian Antioch:

Brothers, children of Abraham, and you God-fearing Gentiles, it is to us that this message of salvation has been sent. The people of Jerusalem and their rulers did not recognize Jesus, yet in condemning him they fulfilled the words of the prophets that are read every Sabbath (Acts 13:26-27).

The large number of prophecies concerning Christ, many of which could be fulfilled only by His enemies, and the minute detail found in many of them, make it impossible for Jesus and His followers to have deliberately set about fulfilling the Messianic prophecies. Thus, the only reasonable explanation is that these prophecies came from the omniscient God who knows the future.

PROPHECIES CONCERNING THE JEWS

The story is told that Frederick the Great of Prussia, who was inclined toward skepticism, once said to one of the pastors of his realm: 'Reverend Sir, what is the most convincing proof you can give me of the divinity of Christ and the inspiration of the Scriptures?' The clergyman hesitated not a moment, 'Sire,' he replied, 'the most convincing proof of the divinity of Christ and the inspiration of the Scriptures that I, or any other person, could give you, is the history of the Jewish people."
Survey Course in Christian Doctrine, Vol III and IV, C.C.Crawford, College Press, 1964, page 279

Truly, the Jews are the most remarkable people in all history. The nation was founded by Abraham, at

the direction of God, for the specific purpose of blessing all mankind by bringing the Son of God into the
world. For centuries the Jews lived with this sense of
purpose. For centuries they longed for the coming
Messiah. To even suggest, that when the Messiah did
come, He would be despised and rejected by His own
people, seemed unthinkable. Yet this was repeatedly
predicted in the Bible, and is exactly what came to
pass.

We have already considered passages from Isaiah 53
and Psalm 22, which describe in detail how Christ
would be rejected and crucified. Psalm 118 contains
this prediction:

> The stone the builders rejected has become the cap-
> stone; the LORD has done this, and it is marvelous in
> our eyes (Psa. 118:22-23).

It was indeed a marvelous thing that the builders,
the Jewish leaders, would reject the very One they
had waited centuries for. Jesus, after telling a parable
that illustrated how the Jews would reject the Son of
God, and how others would take their place, used this
same Psalm to clinch the point:

> Jesus said to them, "Have you never read in the Scrip-
> tures: "'The stone the builders rejected has become
> the capstone; the Lord has done this, and it is mar-
> velous in our eyes'? Therefore I tell you that the king-
> dom of God will be taken away from you and given to
> a people who will produce its fruit. He who falls on
> this stone will be broken to pieces, but he on whom it
> falls will be crushed." When the chief priests and the
> Pharisees heard Jesus' parables, they knew he was
> talking about them (Matt. 21:42-45).

Moreover, Jesus made it clear that the Jews rejection of Him would not be just a temporary misunderstanding, but would continue and would bring terrible consequences for the Jews.

> I say to you that many will come from the east and the west, and will take their places at the feast with Abraham, Isaac and Jacob in the kingdom of heaven. But the subjects of the kingdom will be thrown outside, into the darkness, where there will be weeping and gnashing of teeth (Matt. 8:11-12).

Shortly before His crucifixion, Jesus told His disciples of the coming destruction of their homeland:

> Jesus left the temple and was walking away when his disciples came up to him to call his attention to its buildings. "Do you see all these things?" he asked. "I tell you the truth, not one stone here will be left on another; every one will be thrown down"(Matt. 24:1-2)

Jesus went on to describe the terrible suffering and slaughter that was coming upon the Jews, and then said:

> I tell you the truth, this generation will certainly not pass away until all these things have happened (Matt. 24:34).

The Roman legions moved into Palestine in 66 A.D. and devastated the nation, finally destroying Jerusalem and the temple buildings in 70 A.D. The Jewish historian Josephus tells in great detail of the horrible suffering and slaughter of the Jews — all just as Jesus had predicted. The remaining Jews were scattered throughout the world, but even then their troubles did not end. Fifteen centuries before Christ, Moses had predicted with amazing detail and accuracy, just what would happen.

> Then the LORD will scatter you among all nations, from one end of the earth to the other. There you will worship other gods—gods of wood and stone, which neither you nor your fathers have known. Among those nations you will find no repose, no resting place for the sole of your foot. There the LORD will give you an anxious mind, eyes weary with longing, and a despairing heart. You will live in constant suspense, filled with dread both night and day, never sure of your life (Deut. 28:64-66).

As these, and other prophecies in the Bible warned, the persecution of the Jews has continued down through the centuries. Both night and day, they have dreaded the sound of the heavy boot. And yet, they have continued in their rejection of Jesus, the Son of God, who came in their very own nation, and in accordance with their very own Scriptures.

This spiritual blindness of the Jewish people is one of the greatest mysteries of all history. They are an intelligent, talented nation, justly famous for their spiritual insight. They have repeatedly demonstrated great zeal for God and great courage in defending the truth. Humanly speaking, Jesus Himself is a Jew, as were the apostles and all of the first Christians. Yet, the Jewish leaders and the great majority of the Jewish people, rejected their longed-for Messiah, and continue to do so.

From the perspective of Christian Evidences, the importance of all this is that the whole incredible story was foretold by Jesus, and even by Old Testament prophets. An illustration used by Dr. Crawford in his book cited above, is worth repeating:

I am reminded of a conversation reported to me recently as having taken place between a Christian elder and a young Jew. The two became engaged in conversation riding side by side on a train, and in the course of the talk the subject of religion was introduced. The elder informed the young Jew that he was a Christian, and held the office of elder in a congregation of Christians. Whereupon the Jew said: "I can't understand how you can believe all that stuff about Jesus being the Son of God." Then, after a pause, he added: "Just what are your reasons for believing it, anyway?" "You are one of the reasons," replied the elder. The other looked at him in astonishment for a moment, then asked, "Just what do you mean?" "What I mean is just this," answered the elder, "that one of the reasons why I believe in Jesus Christ is the attitude taken toward Him by you Jews. You reject Jesus. A great many of your people still despise Him. Very few of your people have ever accepted Him as their Savior. And that is exactly the attitude He said you would take. He foretold again and again in His teaching that His own people would reject Him and stumble on in blindness of unbelief. He foretold the desolation of your city and the dispersion of your people among all nations. He foretold the suffering and persecution that you have endured for your rebelliousness. He foretold the forfeiture of your election as the chosen people. And in all these matters your people have fulfilled His predictions in every particular."

As the German pastor told Frederick the Great, the history of the Jewish people is convincing proof of the divinity of Christ and the inspiration of the Bible.

A PROPHECY CONCERNING TYRE

The main city of ancient Tyre was on the mainland, but there was also a fortified city on an island about half a mile off shore. In the 26th chapter of Ezekiel, the prophet foretold the destruction of Tyre by the Babylonians under Nebuchadnezzar, but limited the destruction to the settlements on the mainland. He told in some detail how the siege would be conducted and the city destroyed. Then he made a very unusual prediction:

> They will plunder your wealth and loot your merchandise; they will break down your walls and demolish your fine houses and throw your stones, timber and rubble into the sea (Ezek. 26:12).

The Babylonians broke down the walls and demolished the houses, but left the rubble where it fell. It appeared the last part of Ezekiel's prophecy would never be fulfilled. Why would anyone want to undertake the enormous task of throwing all those stones, timber and rubble into the sea? But about 250 years later, Alexander the Great came with his armies to attack the island city of Tyre. Lacking the ships to attack the Tyrian fleet, Alexander built a causeway out to the island. His soldiers fulfilled Ezekiel's prophecy to the letter, by throwing the stones, timber and rubble of mainland Tyre into the sea.

Many other examples could be given of prophecies concerning the fate of nations and empires and even individuals. Even if the Bible contained only one real example of fulfilled prophecy, that is, one prophecy containing such extraordinary detail as to preclude accidental fulfillment, such as those concerning Jesus, or those concerning the Jews, or the one concerning Tyre, and such prophecy is precisely fulfilled years, and even centuries later, that is a supernatural act — something that could come only from God. Yet the

Bible contains a great volume of such prophecy, much of it already fulfilled. No other book could possibly do this — only the Word of God.

Study Questions

1. Why did God use both miracles and fulfilled prophecy to attest His Word?

2. What did Peter mean when he wrote to early Christians that they had the word of the prophets "made more certain"?

3. What is the most important and abundant group of prophecies in the Bible?

4. Why did Jesus chide His disciples for being surprised and discouraged by His crucifixion?

5. Why did the prophecy that all nations would be blessed by the seed of Abraham seem unlikely to a Jew?

6. Why did Isaiah's prophecies concerning Christ seem contradictory?

7. Give some of the details about the crucifixion of Jesus which David foretold in Psalm 22.

8. Why is it absurd to say that Jesus set about fulfilling all the prophecies concerning the Messiah?

9. Why is the history of the Jews convincing proof that Jesus is the Son of God?

10.What amazing prophecy did Ezekiel make concerning the city of Tyre?

11

THE RESURRECTION, PART ONE

We come now to the very climax of our study; to that key line of evidence that constitutes the heart of the case for the truth of Christianity. We have already considered many lines of evidence which we can see in the universe around us, which we can see within ourselves, and which we can draw from human experience, all of which prove beyond a reasonable doubt that God does exist, that the spirit world is real, and that supernatural events do occur.

We have considered the evidence and arguments against Christianity, and have seen that they fall far short of disproving its claims. We have considered many lines of evidence, both internal and external, including the powerful evidence from fulfilled prophecy, which prove beyond a reasonable doubt that the Bible is the Word of God, and that Jesus is the Son of God. We could rest our case right here, having proved to the satisfaction of most that the claims of Christianity are true.

But even if we had none of the evidence thus far presented, the evidence for the bodily resurrection of Jesus Christ from the dead is, by itself, sufficient to prove our entire case. For not only is the resurrection the most important miracle in the Bible, but also, God, in His wisdom, has given us the strongest evidence for it. People who disbelieve the resurrection do so not because of the evidence, but in spite of the evidence. No other fact of ancient history is so well proven.

In addition to being the most important and the most conclusive line of Christian evidence, the resurrection is one of the two basic truths of the Gospel of Christ, the other being His atoning death. Paul expressed this as follows:

> Now, brothers, I want to remind you of the gospel I preached to you, which you received and on which you have taken your stand. By this gospel you are saved, if you hold firmly to the word I preached to you. Otherwise, you have believed in vain. For what I received I passed on to you as of first importance: that Christ died for our sins according to the Scriptures, that he was buried, that he was raised on the third day according to the Scriptures (I Cor. 15:1-4).

Obviously, if the evidence proves beyond a reasonable doubt that Jesus was raised from the dead, as the Bible says, then it also proves beyond a reasonable doubt that He is the Son of God, that the Bible is the Word of God, and that all the claims of Christianity are true. And that means that the other basic Gospel doctrine, that He died for our sins, is true and we may absolutely rely on it. We may stake our lives on it.

Therefore, the fact of the resurrection is not only the climax of our study of Christian evidences, but also the very climax of all human history. If on that one glorious three day weekend, the Son of God actually died for our sins, and then arose from the grave, giving us the victory over death, then all other events of history are rendered insignificant by comparison. The view a person takes of the resurrection should, if responded to intelligently, determine the whole course of his life.

Prejudice against the resurrection is illogical. Most of it is based on the same bias against miracles that is used against the whole Bible. Paul marveled at this bias in his defense before King Agrippa:

> Why should any of you consider it incredible that God raises the dead? (Acts 26:8).

Certainly the Creator of life can give life. To approach the evidence for the resurrection with a closed mind, denying the possibility of such a miracle, is to deny the existence of God, which we have already seen is unreasonable.

TWO ADMISSIONS UNBELIEVERS HAVE BEEN FORCED TO MAKE

Because of the overriding importance of the resurrection, unbelievers have expended much effort in their attempts to discredit or disprove it. Nevertheless, unbelievers have been forced to admit two highly significant facts: that the tomb was empty and that, from the very beginning of the Church, the Christians believed in the resurrection.

The importance of this is obvious. Had unbelievers been successful in their efforts to date the origin of belief in the resurrection in the second or third century A.D., then they could have dismissed the whole matter as mere legend. But these efforts have been thoroughly refuted by early fragments of the New Testament, by early accounts of secular writers, by early Church practices, and by archeological evidence.

J.N.D.Anderson, OBE LLD, Professor of Oriental Laws and Director of the Institute of Advanced Legal Studies in the University of London, in his book, *Christianity: the Witness of History*, The Tyndale Press, London, 1969, had this to say about the attempts to give a late date to belief in the resurrection:

> The idea that these stories might have been legends rather than lies seems at first sight somewhat more plausible. Had it been possible to date the records a century or two after the event — and repeated attempts to do precisely this have been made by a series of brilliant scholars — the suggestion might have been feasible. But the attempt has decisively failed, crushed under a weight of contrary evidence; and there can be no reasonable doubt that the testimony to the resurrection can be traced back to the very first decade after the event. It seems meaningless, therefore, to speak of legends when we are dealing, not with stories handed down from generation to generation, but accounts given by the eyewitnesses themselves or attributed to them while they were still present to confirm or deny them.

Having been forced to admit that Christians believed in, and preached about, the resurrection from the very first, unbelievers have also had to concede that the tomb was empty. Professor Anderson, in his book cited above, made these further comments:

> So the empty tomb stands, a veritable rock, as an essential element in the evidence for the resurrection. To suggest that it was not in fact empty at all, as some have done, seems to me ridiculous. It is a matter of history that the apostles from the very beginning made many converts in Jerusalem, hostile as it was, by proclaiming the glad news that Christ had risen from the grave — and they did it within a short walk from the sepulchre. Their message could not have been maintained in Jerusalem for a single day, for a single hour, if the emptiness of the tomb had not been established as a fact for all concerned. Any one of their hearers could have visited the tomb and come back again between lunch and whatever may have been the equivalent of afternoon tea. Is it conceivable then, that the apostles would have had this success if the body of the one they proclaimed as risen Lord was all the time decomposing in Joseph's tomb? Would a great company of the priests and many hard-headed Pharisees have been impressed with the proclamation of a resurrection which was in fact no resurrection at all, but a mere message of spiritual survival couched in the misleading terms of a literal rising from the grave?

Having been compelled by the evidence to admit that the tomb was empty, and that belief in the resurrection goes back to the resurrection itself, unbelievers have been forced to devise explanations to account for these two undeniable facts. Because several of these theories have been widely publicized, and may have troubled the faith of some, it is worthwhile to consider them briefly. The weakness and absurdity of these attempted explanations will serve only to emphasize the strength of the evidence for the resurrection.

1. The swoon theory.

According to this theory, Jesus did not die on the cross, but only fainted and then revived in the tomb, and came forth and appeared to some of His disciples who believed He was risen.

The evidence clearly refutes this theory. Death by crucifixion was usually the result of asphyxiation. The weight of the body on the arms caused the chest muscles to compress the lungs and make breathing extremely difficult. By raising the body with his legs, the victim could relieve this pressure and draw air into his lungs. Thus, a man in good physical condition, could fight off death for a considerable time. When the executioners were ready to complete their job, they used a heavy mallet to break the victims legs, who, being then unable to raise his body, quickly suffocated.

Jesus, of course, was not in good physical condition when He was nailed to the cross. Pilate, who did not want to sentence Him to death, had ordered Him scourged, hoping this would satisfy the Jewish leaders. Roman scourging was performed with a multi-thonged whip weighted at the tips with bits of metal or bone. It was designed to rip the skin and flesh from the body and often resulted in the death of the victim. The terrible shock and loss of blood from the scourging, plus the lack of food, loss of sleep, and abuse which He had suffered all night, left Him so weakened that He fell under the weight of the cross. It was obvious that He would not be able to stave off asphyxiation for more than a few hours.

John, the only apostle with the courage to stand near the cross, tells us what happened:

Now it was the day of Preparation, and the next day was to be a special Sabbath. Because the Jews did not want the bodies left on the crosses during the Sabbath, they asked Pilate to have the legs broken and the bodies taken down. The soldiers therefore came and broke the legs of the first man who had been crucified with Jesus, and then those of the other. But when they came to Jesus and found that he was already dead, they did not break his legs. Instead, one of the soldiers pierced Jesus' side with a spear, bringing a sudden flow of blood and water. The man who saw it has given testimony, and his testimony is true. He knows that he tells the truth, and he testifies so that you also may believe. These things happened so that the scripture would be fulfilled: "Not one of his bones will be broken," and, as another scripture says, "They will look on the one they have pierced" (John 19:31-37).

The execution squad was composed of Roman soldiers under the command of a centurion. They had orders to execute Jesus and they were trained to obey orders. They could see Jesus was dead. No doubt His body was motionless, slumped down with the weight on His arms, compressing His lungs, unable to breath. This was the position of a man who is dead, not one who has only fainted. But to be sure, one soldier thrust a spear into Jesus' side. Since He was not pushing His weight up with His legs, there was no need to break the bones. Unknowingly, the soldiers had fulfilled two more Old Testament prophecies.

What happened next is also carefully recorded for us by John:

Later, Joseph of Arimathea asked Pilate for the body of Jesus. Now Joseph was a disciple of Jesus, but secretly because he feared the Jews. With Pilate's permission, he came and took the body away. He was accompanied by Nicodemus, the man who earlier had visited

Jesus at night. Nicodemus brought a mixture of myrrh and aloes, about seventy-five pounds. Taking Jesus' body, the two of them wrapped it, with the spices, in strips of linen. This was in accordance with Jewish burial customs. At the place where Jesus was crucified, there was a garden, and in the garden a new tomb, in which no one had ever been laid. Because it was the Jewish day of Preparation and since the tomb was nearby, they laid Jesus there (John 19:38-42).

Joseph and Nicodemus were Jewish leaders, no doubt intelligent and well educated. In performing the difficult task of removing the body from the cross and wrapping it in the burial clothes with the seventy-five pounds of myrrh and aloes, they would surely have known if the body was still warm and alive and breathing. As it had been to the soldiers, it was obvious to them that Jesus was dead. There is not one shred of evidence to support the suggestion that Jesus only fainted on the cross.

Nor is that the only problem with the "swoon theory." Professor Anderson, in his book cited above, points out even more difficulties:

> But even if, for argument's sake, it is postulated that His life might not have been wholly extinct, is it really likely that to lie for hours in a rock-hewn tomb in Jerusalem at Easter, when it can be distinctly cold at night, would so far have revived Him, instead of proving the inevitable end to His flickering life, that He would have been able to loose Himself from yards of grave clothes weighted by pounds of spices, roll away a stone which three women felt incapable of tackling, and then walk miles on wounded feet?
>
> But it was the sceptic, D.F. Strauss, who, as it seems to me, finally exploded this theory when he wrote: 'It is impossible that a being who had stolen half dead out of the sepulchre, who crept about weak and ill,

wanting medical treatment, who required bandaging, strengthening and indulgence . . . could have given the disciples the impression that he was a Conqueror over death and the grave, the Prince of Life, an impression which lay at the bottom of their future ministry. Such a resuscitation . . . could by no possibility have changed their sorrow into enthusiasm, have elevated their reverence into worship.' Nor could the disciples ever have made such a mistake unless Christ Himself had deliberately exploited their credulity.

2. The Passover plot.

According to this theory, Jesus, Nicodemus, and a few others, conspired to stage the sacrificial death on the cross. A co-conspirator was to be ready at the cross with a spongeful of some narcotic to dull the pain and induce unconsciousness. Then Nicodemus and his helpers were to take the apparently lifeless body and revive Him and pretend that He had arisen. Although the plot was foiled by the spear thrust in His side, Jesus did live long enough for the conspirators to convince the disciples that He had risen from the tomb, after which He was secretly buried.

Of course, there is no evidence to support this theory. It rests on nothing but speculation, and faces many difficulties. Even if the conspirators had not foreseen the spear in the side, they would have expected the Roman soldiers to make certain that Jesus was dead, probably by breaking His legs. They could not have expected to get Him off the cross still alive.

Even if they had been able to get Jesus off of the cross alive, and into the tomb, they would have immediately encountered another problem. The guard, unexpectedly stationed at the tomb, would have prevented them from getting Jesus back out of the tomb.

189

Furthermore, the theory requires that the secret be kept perfectly and permanently by all the co-conspirators, something that human nature makes most unlikely. Nor does there seem to be any reason or purpose for the whole plot. There is no evidence that any of the alleged conspirators gained anything from the deception.

The theory does not explain the numerous appearances of Jesus to persons who supposedly were not aware of the plot — appearances that involved such close contact that there could have been no mistake of identity. Lastly, this theory requires that Jesus be a deceiver, party to a blasphemous falsehood. In view of all that we know about the life and teachings of Jesus, even unbelievers find it hard to accept this. The so-called "Passover Plot" is bizarre speculation, nothing more.

3. The hallucinated woman theory.

A hallucination is the apparent perception of sights, sounds, etc. which are not actually present. By this theory, Mary Magdalene was in love with Jesus and was so devastated by His death that she hallucinated, thinking that she saw Him, and convinced the disciples that He had risen.

In the first place, Mary never could have convinced the disciples of such a thing. Jewish men of that time did not consider women as equals and would have quickly discounted Mary's story. In fact, they refused to believe when at least five women reported their actual encounter with the risen Lord:

> When they came back from the tomb, they told all these things to the Eleven and to all the others. It was

Mary Magdalene, Joanna, Mary the mother of James, and the others with them who told this to the apostles. But they did not believe the women, because their words seemed to them like nonsense (Luke 24:9-11).

In addition, this theory does not explain the numerous appearances that the risen Lord made to others — to the apostles, to several individuals, and even to a crowd of over five hundred at one time. Also unexplained is the fact the the tomb was empty. There is really nothing to be said in favor of this theory.

4. The hallucinated witnesses theory.

By this theory, not just Mary Magdalene, but all of the people who saw the risen Lord, had hallucinations. Since hallucinations are subjective impressions within a persons mind, they do not occur to large numbers of people at the same and in the same way. They usually occur to someone in an emotional or drugged condition, and usually involve something expected and hoped for. The disciples were discouraged and disillusioned after the crucifixion, and certainly were not expecting the resurrection. In fact the first witnesses of the resurrection had difficulty convincing the others. Obviously conditions were not right for any hallucinations, let alone mass hallucinations.

Furthermore, this theory does not explain the fact that the disciples talked with Jesus, touched Him, and ate with Him. Nor does it explain the fact that the tomb was empty. Lastly, it does not explain why the appearances suddenly ceased — which Christians know was because Christ returned to heaven.

5. The vision or spiritual appearance theory.

According to this theory, Jesus did appear to His disciples but only as a spirit or supernatural vision. Note that this theory substitutes one supernatural event for another, which seems pointless. However, it was to head off just such a theory that Jesus ate with the disciples and insisted that they touch Him:

> While they were still talking about this, Jesus himself stood among them and said to them, "Peace be with you." They were startled and frightened, thinking they saw a ghost. He said to them, "Why are you troubled, and why do doubts rise in your minds? Look at my hands and my feet. It is I myself! Touch me and see; a ghost does not have flesh and bones, as you see I have." When he had said this, he showed them his hands and feet. And while they still did not believe it because of joy and amazement, he asked them, "Do you have anything here to eat?" They gave him a piece of broiled fish, and he took it and ate it in their presence (Luke 24:36-43).

It is clear that Jesus caused the disciples to believe in His bodily resurrection, and if it was only His spirit they saw, then Jesus was deliberately deceiving them. As stated before, in view of His perfect life and teaching, few are willing to believe that Jesus was dishonest. In addition, this theory fails to explain the empty tomb.

6. The optical illusion or mirage theory.

This is an attempt to explain the resurrection on naturalistic grounds involving the action of light waves and reflections. However, mirages are not this elaborate. They are hazy, indistinct, and distant. Thus, this theory does not explain the appearances inside rooms, nor the talking, touching, and eating. It does not explain the repeated appearances at different places and to many people. And it does not explain the empty tomb.

7. The mistaken women theory.

According to this theory, the women who went to the tomb on that first Easter morning, being strangers in town, went to the wrong tomb which happened to be empty. A young man who happened to be out there, guessed that they were looking for Jesus and said to them, "He is not here. See where they laid Him," and at the same time pointed to the correct tomb. But the women were so overjoyed that they rushed off without seeing the man point, and convinced the disciples that Christ had risen from the grave. This theory makes use of the following scripture:

> As they entered the tomb, they saw a young man dressed in a white robe sitting on the right side, and they were alarmed. "Don't be alarmed," he said. "You are looking for Jesus the Nazarene, who was crucified. He has risen! He is not here. See the place where they laid him. But go, tell his disciples and Peter, 'He is going ahead of you into Galilee. There you will see him, just as he told you.' " Trembling and bewildered, the women went out and fled from the tomb. They said nothing to anyone, because they were afraid (Mark 16:5-8).

As can be seen, this theory uses only part of what the angel said to the women, particularly leaving out the key statement, "He has risen!" We have already seen that the disciples were reluctant to believe the women, and would not have been convinced by this story. Furthermore, this theory does not explain the

193

numerous eyewitness reports by people who saw Jesus, nor does it explain the empty tomb. If the disciples did not check out the correct tomb, we can be sure the Chief Priests and Pharisees did.

8. The falsehood theory.

This is the claim that the disciples knew Jesus had not risen, but conspired to make the false claim that He had. Note first that this does not explain the empty tomb. The disciples were going everywhere witnessing to the resurrection and the Jewish leaders were alarmed by this preaching and were doing all they could to stop it. Certainly they would have checked the tomb, and if the body was still there they could have quickly disproved the resurrection claims. This they could not do because the tomb was empty.

Also, this theory requires a perfectly kept secret by a large number of people. Not only the apostles, but also many other disciples who claimed to have seen Him, were in on the fraud. Even top secret government information cannot be kept secret when that many people know about it. Furthermore, this theory is inconsistent with the character and conduct of the apostles and many other disciples, as will be pointed out under theory No. 9.

9. Theft of the body by His friends theory.

This is the claim that Jesus' followers came by night and stole His body from the tomb and then claimed He had risen. Note that the tomb was sealed and guarded by soldiers. It is not reasonable to believe that the frighten, disillusioned disciples would face those soldiers and risk breaking an official seal. Nor is it reasonable to believe that a whole guard of soldiers would go to sleep on duty at the same time, and would sleep so soundly that not one was awakened by the noise involved in rolling away the large stone and removing the body. And again, this theory requires a perfectly kept secret by a large number of people. But most importantly, this theory, and also the "falsehood theory" discussed above, are inconsistent with all we know about the character and conduct of the people involved. Comments made by Professor Anderson is his book previously cited are appropriate here:

> First, then, the problem of the empty tomb. The earliest attempt to explain this phenomenon is recorded in Matthew's Gospel, where we are told that the Jewish leaders bribed the guard which had been set to watch the sepulchre to say that the disciples had come by night and stolen the body. But no one, so far as I know, accepts this story today. It would be incredible both in ethics and psychology. Imagine the apostles raiding the tomb by night, stealing the body, burying it furtively in some other place, and then proceeding to foist this miserable fraud upon the world. This would run totally contrary to all we know of them: their ethical teaching, the quality of their lives, their steadfastness in suffering and persecution. Nor would it begin to explain their dramatic transformation from dejected and dispirited escapists into witnesses whom no opposition could muzzle.

10. Theft of the body by His enemies theory.

This is the suggestion that the body was moved to some other location on orders of the Chief Priests or Pilate. But the empty tomb alone would not have convinced the disciples. They would have thought, just as Mary Magdalene did, that someone had removed the body:

They asked her, "Woman, why are you crying?" "They
have taken my Lord away," she said, "and I don't
know where they have put him" (John 20:13).

But Jesus appeared to the disciples numerous times,
talking to them, eating with them, and touching them,
and this, together with the empty tomb, convinced
them beyond any doubt that He was alive.

Furthermore, within a few weeks, the disciples
were going all over Jerusalem preaching the resurrection, much to the dismay of the authorities. If they had
moved the body, they would certainly had said so and,
if necessary, have produced the body itself to stop
such preaching. Christianity would never have gotten
off the ground if its enemies had been able to produce
the body of Jesus.

11. Removal of the body by Joseph of Arimathea.

It has been suggested that Joseph put the body in
his tomb only temporarily and later moved it to
another location. Again, the empty tomb alone would
not have convinced the disciples, and again this
theory does not explain the numerous appearances
which Jesus made to His disciples.

Also, Joseph could not have done this secretly. He
would have needed official permission to open the
sealed tomb, and he would have needed help moving
the body. Thus, even if Joseph had been so devious as
to allow the false doctrine of the resurrection to continue, others would have told what happened. Certainly, the officials who gave permission to open the
tomb would have reported this, and probably would
have required Joseph to reveal the location of the
body so the preaching of the resurrection could be
stopped.

By now, two things should be obvious: 1. That unbelievers have gone to a great deal of effort to explain away the empty tomb and the fact that Christians believed in the resurrection from the very first; and, 2. That these efforts have been completely unsuccessful. All this serves to emphasize the overriding importance of the resurrection, even in the eyes of unbelievers. Even they recognize that, if Jesus rose from the dead, Christianity is true and secular humanism is false.

Admissions against interest are important evidence in the trial of a lawsuit. When your opponent is forced to admit facts which are favorable to your case, and when his attempts to explain away these facts have failed, then you can use these facts as evidence and can build upon them with other evidence. This is what we will do in Lesson 12, where we will proceed with the affirmative evidence for the truth of the Resurrection of Jesus from the dead.

Study Questions

1. Why is the resurrection the most important miracle in the Bible?

2. Explain why the one weekend of the resurrection is the very climax of all human history.

3. Why is it illogical to believe that God cannot raise the dead?

4. Why have unbelievers been forced to admit that the tomb was empty?

5. Why is it important that the historical and archeological evidence shows that Christians believed in the resurrection from the very beginning of the Church?

6. What is the swoon theory and why it it unbeliev-
able?

7. Why is it impossible to explain away the resurrection as hallucinations?

8. Why is it impossible to explain away the resurrection as optical illusions?

9. Why is it unreasonable to believe that the friends
of Jesus stole His body and lied about the resurrection?

10. Why is it unreasonable to believe that the Chief
Priests ordered the body moved and this caused the
disciples to believe in the resurrection?

12

THE RESURRECTION, PART TWO

In this lesson we will consider eight distinct lines of evidence, all pointing to the truth of one vital fact — that Jesus arose from the dead. These eight converging lines of evidence will be more than sufficient to prove the resurrection of Jesus beyond any reasonable doubt.

1. We have excellent eyewitness testimony.
a. The number of witnesses is more than adequate. This can be seen from the partial list of witnesses which Paul provided for us:

> and that he appeared to Peter, and then to the Twelve. After that, he appeared to more than five hundred of the brothers at the same time, most of whom are still

living, though some have fallen asleep. Then he appeared to James, then to all the apostles, and last of all he appeared to me also, as to one abnormally born (I Cor. 15:5-8).

Note especially the appearance to over five hundred people at one time. Paul invites his readers to talk to the eyewitnesses themselves, by advising them that most of the witnesses are still alive.

b. The witnesses were in a position to know the facts. All these witnesses listed by Paul were eyewitnesses. Many of them were in close contact with the risen Lord. They talked to Him, touched Him, and ate with Him. Their observation was sufficient for them to know what they were talking about.

c. The witnesses were competent. They were grown men and women of normal intelligence. The records that we have of their actions and accounts show that they were not easily misled. They were sensible fishermen, practical housewives, and even one tax collector. Their number even included one whose dubiousness was so pronounced, that he was ever after known as "Doubting Thomas."

d. The witnesses were honest and truthful men and women. This is especially important, because it is an accepted rule of evidence that proof that a witness' character for truth and veracity is bad is admissible for the purpose of impeaching his testimony. On this point, we refer to "The Testimony of the Evangelists," written by Simon Greenleaf, Royal Professor of Law at Harvard Law School, and one of the greatest authorities on the law of evidence that the world has known.

And first, as to their honesty. Here they are entitled to the benefit of the general course of human experience, that men ordinarily speak the truth, when they have no prevailing motive or inducement to the contrary. This presumption, to which we have before alluded, is applied in courts of justice, even to witnesses whose integrity is not wholly free from suspicion; much more is it applicable to the evangelists, whose testimony went against all their worldly interest. The great truths which the apostles declared, were that Christ had risen from the dead, and that only through repentance from sin, and faith in Him, could men hope for salvation. This doctrine they asserted with one voice, everywhere, not only under the greatest discouragements, but in the face of the most appalling terrors that can be presented to the mind of man. Their master had recently perished as a malefactor, by the sentence of a public tribunal. His religion sought to overthrow the religions of the whole world. The laws of every country were against the teachings of His disciples. The interests and passions of all the rulers and great men in the world were against them. The fashion of the world was against them. Propagating this new faith, even in the most inoffensive and peaceful manner, they could expect nothing but contempt, opposition, revilings, bitter persecutions, stripes, imprisonments, torments and cruel deaths. Yet this faith they zealously did propagate; and all these miseries they endured undismayed, nay, rejoicing. As one after another was put to a miserable death, the survivors only prosecuted their work with increased vigor and resolution. The annals of military warfare afford scarcely an example of the like heroic constancy, patience and unblenching courage. They had every possible motive to review carefully the grounds of their faith, and the evidence of the great facts and truths which they asserted; and these motives were pressed upon their attention with the most melancholy and terrific frequency. It was therefore impossible that they could have persisted in affirming the truths they have narrated, had not Jesus actually risen from the dead, and had they not known this fact as certainly as they knew any other fact. If it were morally possible for them to have been deceived in this matter, every human motive operated to lead them to discover and avow their error. To have persisted in so gross a falsehood, after it was known to them, was not only to encounter, for life, all the evils which man could inflict, from without, but to endure also the pangs of inward and conscious guilt; with no hope of future peace, no testimony of a good conscience, no expectation of honor or esteem among men, no hope of happiness in this life, or in the world to come.

Never before or since have so many witnesses been so powerfully motivated to be completely honest and truthful in their testimony as were these witnesses to the resurrection. Only a stubborn prejudice against anything supernatural, or a deliberate disregard for the accepted elements of proof, could cause anyone to reject their testimony.

2. The radical change in the lives of the apostles and other early Christians.

When Jesus was arrested, His disciples deserted Him and fled. After His crucifixion they were in hiding, torn by fear and despair. Yet, only a few weeks later, they were going all over Jerusalem, fearlessly proclaiming that Jesus was the Christ, and that He had been raised from the dead. They had been transformed from trembling cowards, into men of the utmost courage. What could have produced such a change? Certainly not a dead Jesus. Only the resurrection of their Master from the dead; only their sure knowledge that He was alive and had given them the victory over death, can explain such a radical change.

Nor was this transformation limited to the apostles.

Many others had suddenly changed from timid followers into bold leaders. Even after persecution of the Church began, and men and women were being dragged off to prison, we are told that Christians preached the Word wherever they went (Acts 8:4). The Roman historian, Tacitus, confirms that after Christ was put to death, the "pernicious superstition" broke out afresh and spread not only through Judea, but even throughout Rome itself.

What motivated these people? To what can we attribute such a radical change? That many of them had seen the risen Christ; that all of them knew the tomb was empty; that they were convinced that their Master was alive and was the Son of God; certainly that would have been motivation enough. Anything less is hard to believe. Here indeed, is compelling evidence, pointing to the truth of the resurrection.

3. *The conversion of many of His enemies.*

The Lord's Church began at Jerusalem on the day of Pentecost, just 50 days after the crucifixion. Just outside the city gates had stood the cross to which Jesus had been nailed. Nearby was the tomb, now empty, in which His body had been laid. It was here at this very place and at this very time, that the Christian Gospel was preached. It was a message concerning facts; recent, public events that many of the hearers had witnessed — the crucifixion and resurrection of Jesus. The audience was composed of Jewish men and women, many of whom had participated in the death of Jesus. The apostles didn't mince words:

> Therefore let all Israel be assured of this: God has made this Jesus, whom you crucified, both Lord and Christ (Acts 2:36).

The response by these Jewish audiences to the apostles preaching, is extremely important to us today. That response was immediate and it was amazing:

> Those who accepted his message were baptized, and about three thousand were added to their number that day(Acts 2:41).

> But many who heard the message believed, and the number of men grew to about five thousand(Acts 4:4).

> Nevertheless, more and more men and women believed in the Lord and were added to their number (Acts 5:14).

> So the word of God spread. The number of disciples in Jerusalem increased rapidly, and a large number of priests became obedient to the faith (Acts 6:7).

Both the Roman historian, Tacitus, and the Jewish historian, Josephus, confirm that large numbers of Jews, in and around Jerusalem, became Christians in the very earliest days of the Church. Remember, that the message being preached to them centered on certain events that had recently occurred, the key event being that Christ had arisen from the tomb. Remember, that the tomb was just outside the city gates, and that among them were many persons who claimed to have seen the risen Lord.

If we can be certain of anything, we can be certain of this: before those people gave up their jobs, their property, their family and friends, their whole way of life, and became persecuted outcasts, they had checked the tomb and knew it was empty, and they had checked the witnesses and found them to be truthful, and they were convinced beyond a reasonable doubt that Jesus had risen from the dead, and was indeed the Christ, the Son of the living God.

Especially can we be thankful for the Jewish priests, a "large number" of whom were "obedient to the faith." These were intelligent, educated men. They held positions that commanded great respect and that gave them lifetime security. Before they gave up all this, how thoroughly they must have investigated the evidence, and how completely convinced they must have been of its truth. They investigated the whole resurrection story for us, and if they were convinced beyond a reasonable doubt of its truth, we too should be so convinced.

4. The empty tomb.

As we saw in Lesson Eleven, even unbelievers have been forced to admit that the tomb was empty. The question is "Why was it empty?" We have already examined every possible explanation that unbelievers could come up with, and have seen that none of them are worthy of belief. The only explanation that is reasonable is the one that the apostles and the other witnesses gave — that He arose from the dead.

One fascinating circumstance concerning the empty tomb, is that the arch-enemies of Jesus, the Chief Priests and Pharisees, themselves took action which served greatly to strengthen the evidence in favor of the resurrection.

The next day, the one after Preparation Day, the chief priests and the Pharisees went to Pilate. "Sir," they said, "we remember that while he was still alive that deceiver said, 'After three days I will rise again.' So give the order for the tomb to be made secure until the third day. Otherwise, his disciples may come and steal the body and tell the people that he has been raised from the dead. This last deception will be worse than the first." "Take a guard," Pilate answered. "Go, make the tomb as secure as you know how." So they went and made the tomb secure by putting a seal on the stone and posting the guard (Matt. 27:62-66).

By this action, the enemies of Jesus were used by God to make the evidence of the empty tomb more convincing for us. They made certain that the body could not be stolen or secretly moved, and thus made certain that the only reasonable explanation of the empty tomb is the resurrection of Jesus by the supernatural power of God.

5. Evidence from secular history and archaeology.

By far the best, the most accurate, and the most credible accounts of the resurrection, are those found in the Bible. No historians were ever more thoroughly tested and found to be true, than were Matthew, Mark, Luke, John, Paul, and Peter. But ancient records of the resurrection are not limited to the Bible. Despite the scarcity of writings this old, we do have several documents and inscriptions from first century writers that confirm the historical fact of the resurrection of Jesus from the dead.

Clement of Rome was a Christian writer, born about A.D. 30 and died about A.D. 100. He knew the Apostle Paul and heard him preach. Clement wrote about the suffering and the faithful preaching of the apostles, saying, "For, having received their command, and being thoroughly assured by the resurrection of our Lord Jesus Christ, they went abroad, publishing that the kingdom of God was at hand."

Polycarp was a Christian writer, born about A.D. 70 and martyred at Smyrna about A.D. 155. He was a disciple of the Apostle John. He wrote about the humility, patience, sufferings, resurrection, and ascension of Christ. Irenaeus wrote that he had heard Polycarp say that his information about Jesus came from eyewitnesses.

Ignatius, another Christian writer, was martyred at Antioch about A.D. 116. He wrote of the resurrection; he wrote that the first day of the week was called the Lord's Day and kept in commemoration of the resurrection; he wrote that the apostles ate and drank with the risen Lord and touched Him; and he attributed to the resurrection the courage and perseverance of the apostles, saying, "They believed, being convinced both by His flesh and spirit; for this cause they despised death, and were found to be above it."

Josephus (A.D. 37-100) was a Jewish historian. As quoted in Lesson Nine, he wrote about Christ as follows,

> . . . and when Pilate, at the instigation of the chief men among us, had condemned Him to the cross, they who before had conceived an affection for Him did not cease to adhere to Him; for on the third day He appeared to them alive again, the divine prophets having foretold these and many wonderful things concerning Him.

Another piece of non-Christian evidence, an archeological find, is described by Michael Green, Registrar, London College of Divinity, in his book, *Man Alive*, Inter-Varsity Press, 1967, as follows:

> The other piece of pagan evidence is even earlier than Josephus. It is called the Nazareth Inscription, after

the town where it was found. It is an imperial edict, belonging either to the reign of Tiberius (A.D. 14-37) or of Claudius (A.D. 41-54). And it is an invective, backed with heavy sanctions, against meddling around with tombs and graves! It looks very much as if the news of the empty tomb had got back to Rome in a garbled form (Pilate would have had to report: and he would obviously have said that the tomb had been rifled). This edict, it seems, is the imperial reaction.

Further archeological evidence of the resurrection, is also reported by Michael Green in another book, *Runaway World*, Inter-Varsity Press, 1968.

A third fascinating piece of very early evidence must have a mention. It has elicited considerable scholarly discussion, but has had little other publicity. The Israeli Professor Sukenik discovered in 1945 a sealed tomb outside Jerusalem, in a suburb called Talpioth. It had escaped spoliation, and its contents were intact. There were five ossuaries, or bone caskets, in the tomb, and the style of their decoration confirmed the indication of a coin found there that the tomb was closed in approximately A.D. 50. On two of these ossuaries the name of Jesus appears clearly; one reads in Greek, 'Jesus, help', the other, in Aramaic, 'Jesus, let him arise'. The theological implications of these crudely scratched inscriptions, written within twenty years of the crucifixion, are truly remarkable. They point to Jesus as the Lord of life, who can help even when a loved one has died. They point to Jesus as the risen Son of God, who can raise the Christian dead from their graves. It would be difficult to imagine any archeological finds which could more clearly illustrate the burning faith of the early church in the Jesus whom many of them had known personally as a historical figure walking the streets of Palestine a few years previously.

In addition to these confirmations from secular

history and from archaeology, it should be noted that no writer or historian of the time, Christian or pagan, recorded any evidence contrary to the resurrection.

6. The Church's existence and practices.

The Christian Church can be traced back to the time of Christ. It began suddenly, shortly after His death, and grew rapidly. It grew in spite of powerful opposition and brutal suppression. The fundamental conviction and message of the Church was that Jesus is the Son of God and is risen from the dead. What motivated these people? Where did they get this message? What caused many of them to change completely their way of life? What caused them to deny themselves and place Jesus first in all that they did? Certainly it was not a dead Jewish rabbi. Without the resurrection none of this could be explained. It would be an effect without a cause.

Furthermore, the new Church met for worship on the first day of the week. They did this because that was their great day — the day Jesus arose from the tomb. Remember these first Christians were Jews, and the Jewish day of rest and worship, going back for many centuries, was the seventh day of the week, because that was the day God rested after finishing the creation. What could have motivated a momentous change such as this? Few tasks are more difficult than changing a deeply ingrained religious practice, and it is hard to imagine a practice more deeply ingrained that the Jewish Sabbath. This was possible only because these people were absolutely certain of the resurrection.

But that is not all. The new Church practiced two very important rites — baptism and communion —

BEYOND A REASONABLE DOUBT

both of which point clearly to the resurrection. Baptism in water pictured the death, burial, and resurrection of Jesus Christ.

> Or don't you know that all of us who were baptized into Christ Jesus were baptized into his death? We were therefore buried with him through baptism into death in order that, just as Christ was raised from the dead through the glory of the Father, we too may live a new life (Rom. 6:3-4).

The communion bread and wine pictured the broken body and shed blood of Jesus, yet, instead of being observed with sorrow and weeping, it was shared joyfully with the living Lord. What transformed the sorrow of the Last Supper and the anguish of the Cross into the joy of Communion? Nothing less than the sure knowledge that, because of the resurrection, the cross represented not a defeat, but an eternal victory.

Independence Day is observed in the United States every fourth of July as the anniversary of the adoption by the Continental Congress of the Declaration of Independence on July 4, 1776. The day was first observed in Boston in 1783, and soon spread to other cities and states until it became a national holiday.

Suppose, back in 1783, the city fathers of Boston had declared a holiday to commemorate the Declaration of Independence, when, in fact, there had been no Declaration of Independence. Of course, the holiday would not have been honored because most people alive would have known it was based on a lie. Or suppose, that in 1876, it was declared that the observance of the holiday would be continued as it had been for the past one hundred years, when, in

210

fact, it had never been observed before. Again, the holiday would not have been honored because most people alive would know that it had not been observed before.

But, since the celebration of Independence Day began when many people were alive who knew that the Declaration of Independence actually happened, and since that celebration has continued every year since then, the fact that we observe Independence Day today is proof that the Declaration of Independence did happen.

Baptism, communion, and Sunday worship are monuments to Christ and His resurrection from the dead. They began with the Church back when many people were alive who had known Jesus and knew the truth of His resurrection from the dead. For nearly 20 centuries, Christians have continued to observe these sacred rites, and they stand today as living proof that Jesus is the Son of God and is risen from the dead. Thus, their continued observance today is proof that Christ did arise from the grave.

7. *The internal evidence of the resurrection accounts.*
Each of the four Gospels gives an account of that first Easter Sunday when Jesus arose from the tomb. When we first read these accounts it appears they are in hopeless contradiction. Matthew says it was Mary Magdalene and the other Mary who went out to the tomb. Mark says it was Mary Magdalene, Mary the mother of James, and Salome. Luke says it was Mary Magdalene, Joanna, Mary the mother of James, and the others with them, and John mentions only Mary Magdalene. Furthermore, they all mention different people to whom Jesus appeared on that day.

Does this mean that these are false reports, made-up by dishonest men to deceive us? On the contrary, this is good evidence that these are truthful accounts, because people who conspire to testify to a falsehood rehearse carefully to avoid contradictions. False testimony appears on the surface to be in harmony, but discrepancies appear when you dig deeper. True accounts may appear on the surface to be contradictory, but are found to be in harmony when you dig deeper.

Such is the case with these Gospel accounts. With further study, the apparent contradictions disappear. For example, all four accounts are in harmony with the following sequence of events: Very early a group of women, including Mary Magdalene, Mary the mother of James, Salome, and Joanna set out for the tomb. Meanwhile two angels are sent; there is an earthquake and one angel rolls back the stone and sits upon it. The soldiers faint and then revive and flee into the city. The women arrive and find the tomb opened; without waiting, Mary Magdalene, assuming someone has taken the Lord's body, runs back to the city to tell Peter and John. The other women enter the tomb and see the body is gone. The two angels appear to them and tell them of the resurrection. The women then leave to take the news to the disciples. Peter and John run to the tomb with Mary Magdalene following. Peter and John enter the tomb, see the grave clothes, and then return to the city, but Mary Magdalene remains at the tomb weeping, and Jesus makes His first appearance to her. Jesus next appears to the other women who are on their way to find the disciples. Jesus appears to Peter; He appears to the two disciples on the road to Emmaus; and then appears to a group of disciples including all of the Eleven except Thomas.

Each of the four Gospel writers simply wrote what he had seen and heard or had learned from witnesses and what the Spirit directed. Had it been their purpose to perpetrate a fraud, they would have been concerned about any apparent contradictions. But since they were concerned only with telling the truth, they did not worry about what others were writing.

Another sure mark of the truth, which we find in the Gospel accounts of the resurrection, are the numerous details of the very type that false accounts would be careful to avoid. For example, it is related of the Lord's appearances to His followers, that at first they did not recognize Him. A false story would never have been made up this way, because it is obvious that this would support an argument that the disciples were mistaken and didn't see Jesus at all. Why did the Gospel writers tell it this way? Because their purpose was simply to tell what happened, and that is the way it happened.

The Gospel accounts tell us that Jesus did not appear to any of His enemies, only to His friends. If these had been written by forgers some two or three centuries after the fact, as has been claimed, they would surely have sought to bolster their case by having Jesus appear to the Chief Priests or Pilate or other witnesses who could not have been accused of prejudice in the Church's behalf. Why does the Bible tell us that He appeared only to His followers? Simply because that is the way it happened.

According to the Bible, the risen Christ only appeared occasionally to His followers over a period of forty days. Surely a forger would have bolstered his case by having Jesus stay with them the whole time. But that isn't the way it happened, so that is not the way the Gospel writers recorded it. When Jesus appeared to Mary Magdalene, He told her, "Do not hold on to me, for I have not yet returned to the Father." Down through the centuries, Christians have wondered just what Jesus meant by this. No forger would have included such a statement without any attempt to explain its meaning. As with all these details, the Gospel writers did not worry about the effect, but simply about telling the truth.

Still another mark of the truth of the Gospel accounts, are the numerous "true to life" details that a forger would not have thought of. John outrunning Peter to the tomb, but Peter going in first; John recognizing Jesus from the boat, but Peter jumping in and swimming to shore; the head cloth lying by itself; the two men returning from Emmaus at night; Mary Magdalene asserting that she would carry the body away; the angel instructing the women to tell the disciples "and Peter." All these are evidence of eyewitness accounts that were truthfully reported.

As Dr. R.A. Torrey once wrote, sometimes in a court of law, the story a witness tells is so artless, so straightforward, so natural, and there is such an entire absence of any attempt at coloring or effect, that his testimony bears weight independently of anything we may know of the character or previous history of the witness. As we listen to his story, we say to ourselves, "This man is telling the truth." The weight of this kind of evidence is greatly increased and reaches practical certainty when we have several independent witnesses of this sort, all bearing testimony to the same essential facts, but with varieties of detail, one omitting what another tells, and the third unconsciously reconciling apparent discrepancies between the two. This is the precise case with the four Gospel narratives of the resurrection of Christ. The Gospel writers do not seem to have reflected at all upon the meaning or bearing of many of the facts which they relate. They simply tell right out what they saw in all simplicity and straight forwardness, leaving the philosophizing to others.

8. The resurrection was a fulfillment of prophecy.

The fact that the crucifixion and resurrection of Christ were foretold in prophecy, is evidence that it all happened according to God's plan, and that His supernatural power was involved, and thus that the resurrection did happen. That these great events did happen according to the scriptures is affirmed by Paul.

> For what I received I passed on to you as of first importance: that Christ died for our sins according to the Scriptures, that he was buried, that he was raised on the third day according to the Scriptures (I Cor. 15:3-4).

In Lesson Ten we discussed the detailed descriptions of Christ's suffering and death written by the prophet Isaiah (Isa.53) and by King David (Ps.22). King David also foretold the resurrection, a thousand years before it happened:

> Therefore my heart is glad and my tongue rejoices; my body also will rest secure, because you will not abandon me to the grave, nor will you let your Holy One see decay (Psa. 16:9-10).

In his great sermon on the day of Pentecost, Peter

emphasized the importance of this prophecy. Because the Holy Spirit had caused David to write this, it was impossible for death to keep its hold on Jesus.

> But God raised him from the dead, freeing him from the agony of death, because it was impossible for death to keep its hold on him. David said about him: "'I saw the Lord always before me. Because he is at my right hand, I will not be shaken. Therefore my heart is glad and my tongue rejoices; my body also will live in hope, because you will not abandon me to the grave, nor will you let your Holy One see decay. You have made known to me the paths of life; you will fill me with joy in your presence.' Brothers, I can tell you confidently that the patriarch David died and was buried, and his tomb is here to this day. But he was a prophet and knew that God had promised him on oath that he would place one of his descendants on his throne. Seeing what was ahead, he spoke of the resurrection of the Christ, that he was not abandoned to the grave, nor did his body see decay. God has raised this Jesus to life, and we are all witnesses of the fact (Acts 2:24-32).

Isaiah, after describing the suffering and death of Jesus in amazing detail, also foretold His return to life:

> After the suffering of his soul, he will see the light of life and be satisfied; by his knowledge my righteous servant will justify many, and he will bear their iniquities (Isa. 53:11).

During His earthly ministry, Jesus repeatedly warned His followers of His coming death and resurrection:

> From that time on Jesus began to explain to his disciples that he must go to Jerusalem and suffer many things at the hands of the elders, chief priests and

teachers of the law, and that he must be killed and on the third day be raised to life (Matt. 16:21).

In fact, Christ's prediction of His resurrection was well known, even to His enemies:

> The next day, the one after Preparation Day, the chief priests and the Pharisees went to Pilate. "Sir," they said, "we remember that while he was still alive that deceiver said, 'After three days I will rise again' " (Matt. 27:62-63).

It has been claimed that the resurrection of Christ was a human invention, dreamed up by His followers in order to salvage the movement after their Leader's unexpected death. But the undeniable fact that the resurrection was prophesied hundreds of years before it happened, and the fact that Jesus openly and repeatedly predicted the resurrection, are proof that it was not a human invention, but was a vital part of God's eternal plan. Truly, as Peter said, it was impossible for death to keep its hold on Him. Truly, Christ is risen!

Study Questions

1. What evidence do we have that the witnesses of the resurrection were truthful?

2. What effect did the resurrection have on the lives and conduct of Jesus' followers?

3. Why is the fact that many of the enemies of Jesus became Christians proof of the resurrection?

4. What did the chief priests and Pharisees do that strengthened the evidence of the empty tomb?

5. What reason did Ignatius give for the apostles fearless attitude toward death?

6. What is the significance of the recent archeological find of a tomb near Jerusalem?

7. Why is the rapid growth of the early Christian Church strong evidence for the resurrection?

8. Why are Sunday worship, baptism, and communion evidence for the resurrection?

9. Why are the apparent contradictions in the four Gospel accounts of the resurrection, actually evidence for the resurrection?

10. Why are the prophecies of the resurrection proof that it was not a human invention?

13

THE CLOSING ARGUMENT

The final step in the trial of a lawsuit, before the case is submitted to the jury, is the closing argument. The lawyers are permitted to address the jury directly, reviewing the evidence, and attempting to show the strength of their case and the weakness of the opponent's case. The length of the argument is limited by the judge, and also by the jury's endurance, so it is not possible to rehash every piece of evidence in a long trial. Instead the skillful attorney will remember the main issues in the case, and will focus on the ultimate purpose of the trial.

In this study of Christian Evidences, our purpose has been to prove beyond a reasonable doubt that the claims of Christianity are true. The key issues upon which we have concentrated are, first, that God does exist; that the spiritual realm is real; and that supernatural events do occur; and then that the Bible is the inspired Word of God; and that Jesus is the Son of God. We have considered many converging lines of evidence which point to the truth of each of the issues. Instead of restating all of these lines of evidence here, our closing argument will be organized by an outline that will be easy to remember and that will emphasize the strength of the case for Christianity, and the weakness of the opposition. The main points in our argument are:

1. Christianity tells us the truth about the universe.

2. Christianity tells us the truth about human beings.

3. Christianity is the truth.

Helping the jury to see the weakness of the opponent's case is a necessary part of a good closing argument. As pointed out in Lesson Two, non-Christians include a wide variety of religions, cults, and "isms". It is impractical to deal with each of these because of the great number of them, and unnecessary because it is only those faiths which can be broadly grouped under secular humanism, that have made a serious attempt to disprove Christianity. Although they may differ on some details, it is fair to include atheists, agnostics, pantheists, evolutionists, deists, and others of like-mind, under secular humanism, because the results they achieve are virtually the same.

Also, in discussing the doctrines and beliefs of humanism, it seems fair to use those that have been set forth in Humanist Manifestos I and II. It is recognized that not every humanist agrees with every detail of these two documents, but these documents do set forth what are probably the most widely held beliefs of humanism. And by quoting directly from Manifestos I and II, we can avoid misstating the claims of our opponent. With this understanding, we proceed with the closing argument.

THE TRUTH ABOUT THE UNIVERSE

The Origin of the Universe

The Bible begins with this simple yet marvelously profound statement: "In the beginning God created the heavens and the earth." In just ten words, seven of them of one syllable, we are told all that we need know about the origin of the physical universe. By one stupendous, supernatural act, God brought into existence from non-existence, time, space, and mass/energy. Of course, we do not understand how He did it. We do not need to understand it. Christians recognize that God's ways are so far above man's ways that it would be foolish arrogance to expect to understand all that He does. What do our opponents have to say about the origin of the physical universe? Humanist Manifesto I also deals with the problem with about ten words: "Religious humanists regard the universe as self-existing and not created." Apparently, by the term "self-existing" they mean that the physical universe has no origin — it has always been here.

This theory that the universe has always been here, was refuted back in Lesson Three. We saw that to deny the existence of the supernatural, and yet claim that something exists without beginning, is inconsistent and unreasonable. Anything that exists without beginning is supernatural. Furthermore, the second law of thermodymanics refutes the idea that the universe is "self-existing." This is the law that tells us that the universe is running down — that energy is being dissipated into space and becoming unusable. Thus the universe had a beginning and is coming to an end. The universe is not eternal. Only the supernatural God is eternal.

The idea of a "self-existing" universe was not satisfying to anyone, including humanists, so Humanist Manifesto II handled the problem differently. It says, "We find insufficient evidence for belief in the existence of a supernatural; it is either meaningless or irrelevant to the question of the survival and fulfillment of the human race. As non-theists, we begin with humans not God, nature not deity."

The dilemma of humanism is obvious. The whole idea and purpose of this faith is to make man the highest thing in the universe — to "begin with humans not God." In order to do this, humanists must eliminate the supernatural, because if the supernatural exists, then something exists that is higher than man. Yet, they cannot deny the existence of the universe, and they cannot conceive of any natural means of bringing the universe into existence. So they dispose of the whole problem by declaring that it is "meaningless or irrelevant."

What a strange position to take. Humanists espouse a religion that purports to show people how to live purposeful lives, yet they assert that it makes no difference whether or not there exists a supernatural Creator who placed us here for a purpose. To a non-humanist it seems that nothing could be more meaningful and relevant "to the question of the survival and fulfillment of the human race" than the existence of a supernatural God who is our Creator. The physical universe is composed of vast reaches of space and contains vast quantities of mass/energy. Christianity tells us that all this had a supernatural beginning – created by a supernatural God. This view is in perfect harmony with the laws of nature, and is satisfying to human reason. Humanism, unable to find any natural means for bringing the universe into existence, avoids the problem by declaring it irrelevant. On this great question, "Where did the universe come from?", a question so basic and so obvious that it occurs even to small children, the opposition utterly fails. Christianity gives the only satisfactory answer we can imagine. Humanism attempts to sweep the issue under the rug.

The Origin of Life
But in seeking the truth about the universe, we must deal not only with the origin of the mass/energy, space, and time that make up the physical universe, but also with the origin of life. Christianity tells us that God is the author of life. This agrees with the laws of nature that say that all life on earth comes from prior life. Life came from the living God, who endowed it with the ability to produce more life.

Humanist Manifesto I states that, "Humanism believes that man is a part of nature and that he emerged as the result of a continuous process." Manifesto II, just assumes that evolution is a proven law of science by declaring, ". . . science affirms that the human species is an emergence from natural evolutionary forces."

Evolution is a vital doctrine of secular humanism. If man got here by special creation, then the highest thing in the universe is not man, but his Creator, and the basic belief of secular humanism is gone. Thus, humanists are stuck with evolution. As the evidence against evolution continues to mount, it is obvious that evolution is becoming an embarrassment to humanism. The weakness of their position is exposed by the fact that, unable to answer the evidence for creationism, they have been forced to turn to the Federal Courts to suppress the teaching of creation science in the public schools. For people who espouse the free exchange of ideas, and profess to abhor censorship of any kind, this is indeed a bitter pill to swallow.

As shown in Lessons Six and Seven, the evidence against evolution is overwhelming. We saw the absurdity of the supposed spontaneous generation of life in a "prebiotic soup", and of the supposed sudden appearance of whole new species as "hopeful monsters." We saw that the fossil record, which evolutionists had counted on for their main support, has instead testified against them. We considered instinctive behavior so complex and bizarre, as to preclude any possibility that it developed by accident. And we heard Dr. Michael Denton, the molecular biologist, tell how this new science, which evolutionists had eagerly hoped would support their cause, has also become a witness for the other side.

Secular humanism cannot explain the origin of the physical universe. Instead, they attempt to dismiss this vitally important issue, by saying it is irrelevant. Secular humanism cannot explain the origin of life. Since 1859, they have expended enormous resources attempting to explain life by supposed evolutionary processes. They have failed. Today the theory of evolution is weaker and far less believable than when

Darwin first propounded it. Christianity explains the origin of the universe in the only reasonable and satisfactory way. God did something that is beyond our ability to comprehend. He brought the whole vast universe into existence from non-existence. "In the beginning God created the heavens and the earth." And Christianity explains the origin of life in the only reasonable and satisfactory way. Life did not arise accidentally from dead chemicals. The living God is the Author of life. Truly, Christianity tells us the truth about the universe.

THE TRUTH ABOUT HUMAN BEINGS

The Christian View of Man
The truth which Christianity tells us about human beings consists of two basic facts. First, human beings are created in the image of God:

> Then God said, "Let us make man in our image, in our likeness, and let them rule over the fish of the sea and the birds of the air, over the livestock, over all the earth, and over all the creatures that move along the ground." So God created man in his own image, in the image of God he created him; male and female he created them (Gen. 1:26-27).

Since God is Spirit (John 4:24), being created in His image means that man also is spirit. Throughout the Bible, human beings are treated as spiritual beings. The physical body is not all there is to us. We are both body and spirit, and the spirit lives on after the body dies.

The other basic truth which the Bible tells us about human beings is that we have fallen from our original good condition. Part of being human is having a free

225

will, that is, the power to choose, and beginning with the first humans, we have chosen to rebel against our Creator. By thus cutting ourselves off from God, we have allowed evil influence into our lives and have corrupted human nature:

> Therefore, just as sin entered the world through one man, and death through sin, and in this way death came to all men, because all sinned . . . (Rom. 5:12).

> As it is written: "There is no one righteous, not even one; there is no one who understands, no one who seeks God. All have turned away, they have together become worthless; there is no one who does good, not even one" (Rom. 3:10-12).

The great theme of the Bible is the story of man's redemption from this lost condition. Even though his nature is corrupted, man is still created in the image of God, and thus, is of great value in the eyes of God, and is worth saving.

The Humanist View of Man

Secular humanism paints a very different picture of man. *Humanist Manifesto I* has this to say:

> Second: Humanism believes that man is a part of nature and that he has emerged as the result of a continuous process.

> Third: Holding an organic view of life, humanists find that the traditional dualism of mind and body must be rejected.

Humanist Manifesto II states it this way:

> But we can discover no divine purpose or providence for the human species. . . .

Modern science discredits such historic concepts as the "ghost in the machine" and the "separable soul." Rather, science affirms that the human species is an emergence from natural evolutionary forces. As far as we know, the total personality is a function of the biological organism transacting in a social and cultural context.

Thus, humanism tells us that a human being is nothing but an accidental combination of chemicals. By chance, some chemicals in some ancient sea came alive, and through a long series of random accidents, became human beings. There was no intelligence behind any of this; no one planned any of it; there was no meaning or purpose to any of it.

The logical result of the humanist view of man is determinism — the doctrine that we do not choose or control what we do because our actions are entirely determined by external forces. If we are nothing but chemicals, there is no one there to make choices or to control what we do. Our behavior is nothing but chemical reactions.

Francis A. Schaeffer presented the contrast between the two views of human beings, as follows: *Death in the City*, Inter-Varsity Press, 1969.

Increasingly educated, twentieth-century men tend to emphasize some sort of determinism. Usually it is one of two kinds: chemical determinism (such as the Marquis de Sade put forward and as Francis Crick maintains today) or psychological determinism (such as that emphasized by Freud and those who follow him). In the former, man is a pawn of chemical forces. In the latter, every decision that a man makes is already determined on the basis of what has occurred to him in the past. So whether it is chemical determinism or psychological determinism, man is no longer responsible for what he is or does, nor can he be active in making significant history. Man now is no more than part of a cosmic machine.

The Bible's view of man could not be more different. Romans 1:21-22 says, "When they knew God, they glorified Him not as God, neither were thankful; but became vain in their reasoning, and their foolish heart was darkened. Professing themselves to be wise they became fools." The whole emphasis of these verses is that man has known the truth and deliberately turned away from it. But if that is so, then man is wonderful: he can really influence significant history. Since God has made man in His own image, man is not caught in the wheels of determinism. Rather man is so great that he can influence history for himself and for others, for this life and the life to come.

Which View of Man Fits Reality?

Although the humanistic belief that human beings are nothing but accidental combinations of chemicals, leads inexorably to chemical determinism, humanistic philosophers (with the exception of the Marquis de Sade) do not live that way. In fact, sometimes they are unable even to talk that way. *Humanist Manifesto II* contains this statement:

> Fifth: The preciousness and dignity of the individual person is a central humanist value. Individuals should be encouraged to realize their own creative talents and desires. We reject all religious, ideological, or moral codes that denigrate the individual, suppress freedom, dull intellect, dehumanize personality. We believe in maximum individual autonomy consonant with social responsibility. Although science can account for the causes of behavior, the possibilities of individual freedom of choice exist in human life and should be increased.

That certainly doesn't sound like they are talking

about accidental combinations of chemicals. What could be so precious and dignified about a couple of dollars worth of chemicals? And how do chemicals realize creative talents or exercise social responsibility? If we are nothing but chemicals, how can "possibilities of individual freedom of choice" exist? Although humanists say that they reject such concepts as the "ghost in the machine", even they are forced to think of humans as more than chemicals, because the humanistic view of man just does not fit reality.

Human beings are precious and do possess dignity, for one reason only — we are created in the image of God. Human beings can realize creative talents and can exercise social responsibility, for one reason only — God gave us those abilities. We can be creative because He gave us a sense of beauty, and we can be responsible because He gave us the power to choose, and a conscience to tell us we ought choose what we believe to be right. None of these things belong to chemicals. They are attributes of spiritual beings, created in the image of God.

According to the scientific method, a theory that does not test out is discarded. By that standard, the humanistic view of human beings should be thrown out. It does not fit what we see in ourselves and in others. But the Christian view of man, created in the image of God, and thus capable of great goodness, but fallen, and thus often guilty of great meanness, fits perfectly with what we see in ourselves and in others.

Again the opposition fails to give a consistent and believable answer to a simple and basic question, "What is a human being?" The humanistic-evolutionary doctrine that life appeared by chance in a ancient chemical broth, and developed by chance into human beings, can only mean that humans are nothing but chemicals and human behavior is nothing but chemical reactions. But that doctrine does not fit reality. We all can see in ourselves and in others, attributes that do not belong to chemicals. We know that the real person is something more. The real person is the God-given spirit. Christianity tells us the truth about human beings.

CHRISTIANITY IS THE TRUTH

We have seen so far in this closing argument, that Christianity, speaking through the Bible, tells us the truth about the universe and tells us the truth about human beings. "Where did the universe come from?" and "What is a human being?" are perhaps the two most basic questions that have puzzled philosophers through the centuries. Humanism, despite all the education and scholarship of its leaders, has failed to provide believable answers. Christianity gives answers that are entirely satisfactory to both reason and science. Surely there is a strong presumption that a religion that can do that is true.

But there remains a great deal more evidence to support the truth of Christianity. The evidence that makes Christianity absolutely unique, that makes it the true, and only true, religion from God, is the evidence showing that the Bible is the inspired Word of God, and the evidence showing that Jesus is the Christ, the Son of God.

The Bible is the Word of God
As we saw in Lessons Three and Four, it is possible

to know many things about God from reason and nature. But we know a great deal more about Him because He has revealed it to us. He has intervened in human history, He has revealed His will in various ways, and He has even come here in human form. As is reasonable to expect, God has caused all this to be written down so we would have a permanent record of His revelation, and so we would have true and objective standards to guide our lives and worship. This written record, of course, is the Bible.

Since the Bible records God's dealing with man and His intervention in human affairs, it records many supernatural events. An ill-founded bias against anything supernatural has caused many people to reject the Bible. We have already seen that God does exist, that it is impossible to explain the universe without Him, and since He does exist, that supernatural events are possible. Furthermore, we have seen that the supernatural is probable, in fact necessary, because, if men are to accept God's revelation, it must be authenticated by some evidence of God's power, that is, by miracles.

When we put aside the unreasonable bias against miracles, and look at the Bible with open minds, we see the most remarkable Book the world has ever known. We note first that the Bible repeatedly claims to be from God. Written by some forty different men over a span of at least fifteen centuries, we marvel at its unity of theme and purpose. We are surprised at the Bible's frankness in recording the weakness and misconduct of its greatest heroes. We are impressed by its amazing brevity and lack of coloring. We recognize the mark of true accounts in the Bible's undesigned coincidences and record of familiar details.

When we compare the Bible to contemporary historical records, we find only confirmation, no contradictions. We note that the Bible not only avoids the scientific errors of other ancient writings, but that it actually anticipated many scientific discoveries by many centuries. We are astonished by the numerous archeological discoveries of fragile artifacts that have been preserved for two or three thousand years, and which confirm statements found in the Bible.

We find conclusive proof that the Bible is from God in the "prophetic word made more sure." Prophecies containing minute detail and made a thousand or more years before being exactly fulfilled, could only have come from the mind of God. One such fulfilled prophecy is proof of divine intervention. The Bible contains many. Most of all, we are convinced of the inspiration of the Bible by Jesus, the central character of the Bible, who put His stamp of approval on this great Book.

All these converging lines of evidence point to one vital fact – the Bible is the inspired Word of God. The Bible, the only book that tells us the truth about the universe, and the only book that tells us the truth about human beings, is from God, and therefore is completely true and infallible. It follows, because the Bible tells us so, that Christianity is the truth.

Jesus is the Son of God

The central claim of Christianity is that God came to earth in human form; taught the most wonderful teachings humans have ever heard; demonstrated God's love and authenticated His teachings by performing many miracles; offered Himself as the Lamb of God, the perfect sacrifice for human sin; and then gave us the eternal victory by His resurrection from the dead. If this claim is true, then the central claim of Christianity is also the central event of all history. Nothing else can even remotely approach it in importance.

God, in His wisdom, gave us plenty of evidence to prove beyond a reasonable doubt that all of the claims of Christianity are true. The evidence is overwhelming that Jesus is the Son of God. Without a doubt, He has had far more effect on human history and the lives of people, than anyone else who has lived on earth. If He were only a peasant carpenter, without formal education, without social standing, without ever holding any office or position of authority, merely going about in a small area teaching for three short years, and then executed as a common criminal, how could He have had such a profound effect on the human race? He claimed to be the Son of God and made many statements that make sense only if He is God. Thus, it is correct to say that He was either dishonest, or deranged, or what He claimed to be. But He was far too good to be dishonest, and far too wise to be deranged.

In Lesson Ten we saw that the Old Testament contains many prophecies concerning the coming Messiah, which were exactly fulfilled in the life of Jesus. These prophecies, made many centuries before Christ, contain such minute detail as to make accidental fulfillment impossible. Some of them were fulfilled by His enemies, making deliberate fulfillment impossible. Consider again the prophecies concerning Christ discussed in Lesson Ten. Remember, these are only a few of the approximately three hundred such prophecies in the Old Testament. The only reasonable explanation is that the prophecies came from the mind of God, and the One who fulfilled them is the Son of God.

Fulfilled prophecy alone is sufficient to prove beyond a reasonable doubt that Jesus is the Son of God. His matchless teaching, far above anything produced by human minds, and the many miracles which He performed during His ministry, are sufficient to prove that He is the Christ. Remember, the apostles preached about these things while thousands of people who had witnessed them, were still alive and could have contradicted them had the apostle's claims been false.

> Men of Israel, listen to this: Jesus of Nazareth was a man accredited by God to you by miracles, wonders and signs, which God did among you through him, as you yourselves know (Acts 2:22).

But the greatest proof of all remains. It is fair to say that the resurrection of Christ from the dead, is alone enough to prove all of the claims of Christianity, because His resurrection proved Him to be, as even doubting Thomas cried out, "My Lord and my God!" (John 20:28). Thus, we can rely on everything Jesus said as being the perfect truth. And we can rely on everything the Bible says, because Jesus gave the Bible His approval.

Of course, it is no accident that we have such overwhelming proof of the truth of the resurrection. God does not call us to a blind faith, but to an intelligent faith. He wants our faith to be firmly grounded on sound evidence and historical fact. So, in addition to all the other evidence which He has given us, He made absolutely sure that no honest seeker for the truth need remain in doubt, by giving us sure proof of the resurrection.

God gave us a large number of competent, credible, witnesses who are clearly worthy of our belief. He left for us ample evidence of the amazing transformation of the lives of the early Christians, which could have been caused only by a risen Lord. He left for us the empty tomb, just outside the gates of Jerusalem, a problem that unbelievers have never solved. We have considered the conversion of thousands of Christ's former enemies, intelligent men and women who were there at the very time and place of the resurrection, and who never would have made the great sacrifices involved in becoming Christians, unless they were convinced beyond a reasonable doubt that Christ is risen.

We have looked at the writings of secular historians and at artifacts discovered by archaeologists that confirm the resurrection. God gave us the Church which, with its worship and practices, established immediately after the resurrection, is a living memorial to Christ and His resurrection. We have examined the Biblical accounts of the resurrection and have seen that they bear all of the marks of true records. And we have seen that Christ arose according to the Scriptures, according to Old Testament prophecy and according to His own repeated predictions, made in the presence of many who there to witness the fulfillment.

All of these converging lines of good sound evidence point inescapably to one great fact — Jesus did arise from the dead and thus He is the Christ the Son of God. And this great fact of the resurrection is itself a powerful line of evidence which, together with all the other lines of evidence considered in this study, converge to prove that Christianity is the true religion from God.

A favorite statement often made by lawyers in their closing arguments to the jury is, "You were not required to leave your common sense behind you when you came into this courtroom." By this they mean that there is nothing illogical about the elements of proof, but that it is all based on good common sense. Likewise, it is not necessary to abandon your common sense when you consider the claims of Christianity, for those claims are amply supported by sound evidence and the facts of history.

The Bible contains many wonderful promises pertaining both to this life and to the life to come: that Christians can rejoice under any kind of circumstances; that all things work for good for those who love God; that Jesus came that we might have eternal life; that Jesus has gone to prepare a place for us; that in the coming ages, the all-wise, all-powerful, God is going to show the riches of His grace in kindness to us. How grateful we should be that we do not have to abandon our common sense in order to lay hold of these promises. We do not have to take an irrational leap of faith. God has given us the evidence. Christianity is the truth.

Study Questions

1. Why does proof of the truth of Christianity necessarily disprove all other religions and all cults?

2. What facts show that secular humanism is the main opposition to Christianity in America today?

3. Why is it inconsistent to deny the existence of the supernatural, and yet to claim that the universe is "self-existing?"

4. Why have humanists now taken the position that the existence or non-existence of anything supernatural is "meaningless or irrelevant?"

5. Why is evolution a vital doctrine of humanism?

6. What two basic truths does Christianity tell us about human beings?

7. What is chemical determinism and why does the humanist view of man lead to this?

8. How does the humanistic view of man compare to reality?

9. Why is the resurrection, even by itself, enough to prove all the claims of Christianity?

10. Why is the idea of an "irrational leap of faith" contrary to the teaching of the Bible?

Index of Subjects

A

Abram, all peoples blessed through, 167-168
action, Bible calls for, 161
admissions against interest, 197
age of Earth, 76-81
Alexander the Great, 178
ancient historians, 151-156, 206-207
Anderson, J.N.D., 184, 185, 188-189, 195
anthropomorphism, 73-74
appearance of age, creation requires, 79
Aquinas, Thomas, 47-48
archaeological finds, 156-160, 207-209
Atlas, myth of, 43
atomic theory, foretold, 150-151

B

Bare, Garland, 61-62
Barnes, Thomas, 26
beauty, argument from, 49-51
Belshazzar, archaeological find concerning, 159
Bible
-action called for by, 161
-approved by Jesus, 142-143
-attested by God, how, 165-166
-brevity of, 133-136
-claim to be from God, 126-128
-contemporary accounts given, 160
-contradictions, apparent, 211-213
-external evidence, 146-162

-familiar details of, 136-140, 213-215
-frankness of, 132-133
-historical accuracy, as to
-ancient histories, 151-156
-archaeological finds, 156-160
-historical standards, 160-162
-internal evidence, 126-143
-Jesus central character, 140-142
-lack of coloring, 133-136
-prophecy as proof of, 165-179
-public events recorded, 161
-scientific accuracy, as to
-atomic theory, 150
-First Law of Thermodynamics, 148
-physical body of man, 149
-psychosomatic illness, 149
-Second Law of Thermodynamics, 148
-suspension of Earth, 149
-uniqueness of man, 148-149
-water cycle, 150
-wind currents, 150
-specific details given, 161
-undesigned coincidences of, 136-140
-unity of, 128-132
-weakness of leaders revealed, 132-133
-Word of God, 230-232
Biogenesis, Law of, 95-99
Botta, Paul, 159

239

Index of Scriptures